D. Caroline Coile, Ph.D.

Australian Shepherds

Everything about Purchase,
Care, Nutrition, Behavior,
and Training

With full-color photographs

Illustrations by
Michele Earle-Bridges

BARRON'S

²CONTENTS

History of the Australian Shepherd 5

Early History 5
Later History 6
AKC Recognition 7
Temperament 8

Obtaining an Australian Shepherd 13

Finding an Aussie 13
Custom Choices 20
AKC or ASCA Registration 23

Australian Shepherds as House Pets 25

Accessories for Aussies 25
Safety Measures 26
Housing 27
Fencing 28
Housebreaking 29
Behavior Problems 32

Training Australian Shepherds 37

Training Tips 37
Basic Obedience 39
Canine Good Citizen Test 43

Feeding Your Australian Shepherd 45

Feeding Basics 45
Nutrition Basics 46
Avoiding Fat 48
Feeding Schedules 50
Water 51

Preventive Health Care 53

Health Checks 53
External Parasites 54
Skin Problems 56
Internal Parasites 57
Vaccinations 59
Neutering and Spaying 60
HOW-TO: Grooming 62

Health Problems 65

Choosing a Veterinarian 65
Blood Work 65
Emergency Situations 65
Sickness 70
Giving Medication 73
HOW-TO: First Aid 74

Training for Stock Work 77

Preliminary Training 77
Basic Stock Work 79
Advanced Stock Work 81
Teamwork 83

Activities with Your Australian Shepherd 85

Herding Competitions 85
Obedience Trials 86
Tracking Trials 87
Agility Trials 88
Conformation Shows 89
Community Service 91

Safety and Activities 93

Protecting Your Pet 93
Walking and Jogging 93
Finding a Lost Dog 94
Travel 94
HOW-TO: Lameness 98

The Older Aussie 101

Changes in Your Aussie 101

Living with an Older
Aussie 101

Saying Farewell 103

The Australian Shepherd Standard 105

The ASCA Standard 105

Information 109

Index 110

HISTORY OF THE AUSTRALIAN SHEPHERD

The sky has turned an ominous mottled slate. The wind whips the dry grasses into an undulating sea, occasionally punctuated with whitecaps. A lone figure stands apart, interrupting the howl of the wind with a long whistle. A shape, the same color as the sky, explodes from the sea of grass, sailing across the plain toward the white forms, which now come to life and begin to move. Here and there, the shape darts, always predicting the movements of the forms, pressing them into an ever-smaller gathering, until finally the group moves toward the lone figure on the hill. The wail of the wind, the sound of the whistle, the bleating of the sheep, the barking of the dog, the rumble of hoofbeats—this is the song of the Australian Shepherd. It is a song accompanied by a graceful dance of dog and sheep, orchestrated by the shepherd. It is a dance that is not only a thing of beauty, but a necessity of ranch life. It is a dance that has been performed for generations.

Early History

Exactly how humans and dogs first joined forces is lost in time, but their partnership has

Today's Aussie results from generations of breeding for a dog that could perform as herder, companion, and sometimes even protector.

flourished and evolved since then until the dog gradually became the most versatile of human helpers. One of the most essential roles throughout history has been that of a helper with livestock. Some breeds specialized in guarding the stock from marauding predators, others in herding the stock, and some combined both talents. Even among the herding breeds, dogs specialized in working cattle or sheep, or in driving or gathering. Thousands of generations of selection produced dogs so perfectly suited for every type of herding situation that they have never been surpassed by modern technology.

When European settlers came to America they brought with them the livestock and stock-tending dogs of their native lands. These breeds probably included the English Shepherd, Dorset Blue Shag, Cumberland Sheepdog, and Smithfield Sheepdog from England, the Scottish Collie from Scotland, the Glenwherry Collie from Ireland, the Welsh Grey Sheepdog from Wales, the Bouvier des Flandres from France, as well as several breeds from Germany and Spain. Just as America was a melting pot for human immigrants, so the various breeds began to interbreed.

The Gold Rush

Most of the sheep and sheepdogs remained in the eastern parts of America, where conditions were not that different from those of Europe.

Western America posed a very different situation, however. Here the land was harsh, intensely hot in the arid southern regions and bone-chillingly cold in the North. Settlers from Spain populated the southern and California coastal regions, and with them came their Spanish shepherd dogs. Still, their numbers were low and these breeds remained distinct from their counterparts back East. The situation might have remained except for one word: "Gold!"

The rush was on, and so was the genesis of the Australian Shepherd. Until that time the vast and rugged areas of the far western regions of America had attracted only the most adventurous of settlers, but with the advent of the Gold Rush, people flocked to California. Huge flocks of sheep were driven from the Midwest and Southwest, and shipped from the East and abroad. As the sheep population grew, so did the sheepdog population. The dogs reflected the nationalities of their people, so most of the midwestern and eastern sheepdogs were of British stock, whereas those from the Southwest were of Spanish descent. Most of the imported sheep came from Australia, and many were accompanied by Australian stockdogs, which were in turn derived from British stock. Australian herding dogs had already begun to be selected for their ability to work in much more rugged conditions than their European ancestors, and these conditions more closely resembled those of the American West.

The sheepherders of the time did not care about their dogs' ancestry or looks; they depended upon them for their livelihood and simply bred the best workers to the best workers. Gradually, a strain of dogs emerged that was adept at handling stock in all types of rough terrain through blinding storms, sweltering heat, and frigid cold. These dogs had to react instantly to movements of the sheep as well as the commands of their sheepherder, but also had to be able to act independently and think for themselves. So was born the Australian Shepherd.

Later History

Why would this breed that was born and bred on American soil be dubbed "Australian"? The answer to this remains a mystery. One popular theory holds that these dogs accompanied Basque sheepherders arriving from Australia and formed the nexus of the herding dogs of the American West. However, most of the Basque sheepherders who arrived during the nineteenth century did so by way of Latin America and Europe; by the time Basque immigrants arrived en masse from Australia in the early twentieth century, the Australian Shepherd had already been established. Thus, the secret of the Australian Shepherd's name goes beyond the Basque immigrants, and may lie with the Australian immigrants who arrived with their sheep and dogs in the mid 1800s. Perhaps their dogs had a distinctive look that set them apart from the other sheepherding dogs of the time. Some conjecture exists that the Australian imports may have included a large number of merle-colored animals, and that people began to refer to any merle-colored shepherd as an Australian Shepherd. The origin of the Australian name for this quintessential American dog will almost certainly remain a mystery.

Legend has it that the Native Americans of the West held these "ghost-eyed" dogs to be sacred, and avoided them and their people. Like its name, the origin and history of the Australian

Shepherd will likely always be cloaked in doubt, but its uncanny ability to predict and control the movements of livestock, as well as capture the hearts of humans, might very well be evidence that the Native Americans were right.

The Australian Shepherd continued to prosper in the West, proving itself an invaluable ranch hand. These dogs had to be quick, hardy, obedient, intelligent, weatherproof, and tireless. Generations of selection for working ability produced the American West's preeminent sheepdog, yet it was still more of a strain or type than a breed. The dogs were relatively unknown outside of the West or off the ranch. The situation changed with a man named Jay Sisler, whose Aussies showed they could turn their intelligence and athleticism to other areas. They became hits as trick dogs in touring rodeos of the 1950s and 1960s. The big break came when they were given roles in several films, most notably the Disney films *Run Appaloosa Run* and *Stub: The Greatest Cowdog in the West.* So astounding were these dogs that moviegoers and dog fanciers who had never seen such feats or dogs traveled to the West to see them in action, often returning with one of their own. Many of today's Aussies can be traced back to Sisler's rodeo dogs.

Even before the Aussie found fame on the big screen, a few dog fanciers, mostly in the western United States, had discovered these impressive dogs. In 1957 they formed the Australian Shepherd Club of America (ASCA). In that same year the National Stock Dog Registry (NSDR) became the official registration body for the breed. The NSDR's influence continued to help ensure that the Aussie would remain a functional herding dog rather than a dog bred primarily for beauty. As the breed gained in popularity, however, more fanciers wanted to also enjoy competition in obedience and conformation forums, and in 1971 the ASCA took over as the official registry. Aussies registered with the ASCA could take part in a wide variety of competitive venues, making the Aussie more attractive to fanciers who were not in a position to train their dogs for herding trials. In 1977 a breed standard by which the conformation of Aussies could be objectively evaluated was approved (see pages 105–108). For some Aussie fanciers, the next logical step was to seek American Kennel Club (AKC) recognition.

AKC Recognition

Not all breed fanciers wanted AKC recognition, however, so when it was proposed in 1985, the ASCA declined to pursue AKC affiliation. Many club members feared that the emphasis on conformation competition that often accompanies AKC recognition would divide the breed into show and herding types, rather than the all-purpose Aussie they valued. In addition, the increased popularity that is sometimes created by the words "AKC registered" was worrisome, as the Aussie was not a breed for everyone. Nonetheless, several Aussie breeders felt that AKC recognition would benefit the breed, and in 1991 they formed the United States Australian Shepherd Association (USASA). They modified the ASCA standard and petitioned the AKC for full recognition, which was granted in 1993. The situation has left the Australian Shepherd with two parent clubs in the United States: the original and largest is the ASCA; the official AKC club is the USASA.

The Aussie has since become a major contender in the herding group at AKC dog shows,

The North American Shepherd is a miniature version of the Australian Shepherd, reaching a height of only about 16 inches (41 cm).

and a strong competitor at AKC herding trials. It is still a valued working dog and staunch herding trial contender at non-AKC events. Despite an influx of fanciers interested primarily in show, the Aussie has kept its base of breeders who believe the Aussie should be, above all, a working stockdog with exceptional temperament.

The Aussie has continued to grow in popularity as a pet, but not always for the good of the dogs, their owners, or the breed as a whole. Although the breed seems to have withstood many of the detrimental aspects of AKC recog-

nition, the ASCA was definitely right about one thing: The Aussie is not the breed for everyone.

Temperament

As the Australian Shepherd finds its way into more and more homes, it is also finding its way into more unsuitable situations. Think carefully before asking an Aussie to share your life. Aussies are sensitive dogs and will not understand why you have abandoned them to a pen in the yard, the garage, or the pound. Too often, prospective dog owners select their new dog based upon its physical characteristics, with the assumption that all dogs act alike. They do not. Generations of selection have seen to that. Behavior is malleable, but dogs are born with a propensity to act in certain ways dictated by their genes. Not all dogs within a breed act the same, but most dogs within a breed have a tendency to act in certain ways, especially if those traits are important ones for doing the job for which the breed was developed. Don't get an Aussie and expect it to act like a retriever—that's just not in its genes. And besides, to try to change the breed would be to deprive it of its heritage.

Genetic Heritage

So what is the Australian Shepherd's genetic heritage?

✔ The Aussie is an energetic, playful, intelligent, biddable dog that is happiest when it has a job to do.

✔ It can be a well-mannered and calm dog in the house as long as it is given adequate exercise—mental and physical—throughout the day.

✔ It is a devoted companion, loving and loyal to its family.

✔ It has a protective nature, and will guard its family bravely.

✔ It is an excellent watchdog, and a pretty good protection dog. This is not a dog that will throw itself on strangers in greeting; instead, it is reserved with those it doesn't know. A few Aussies go beyond "reserved" and are instead shy with strangers.

✔ The Aussie generally gets along well with other dogs and pets.

Australian Shepherds are unrivaled at dividing their time as family companions and ranch workers.

Herding Tendencies

Herding is the breed's reason for being, and what truly defines the Aussie. This urge to herd is essential for people wanting an Aussie as a stockdog or herding competitor, but it can be an irritating trait to people looking for the traditional suburban pet. Lacking stock, these dogs will sometimes try to herd other pets (which may cause conflicts if the other pet becomes sufficiently annoyed) or children (which can scare those unfamiliar with the dog's behavior), and some have a tendency to chase moving vehicles. Sometimes the dog will nip at heels or grasp a hand in its mouth, causing some people to believe the dog is acting aggressively. Herding inappropriate objects is not a universal problem and it can be trained out if done early and consistently. After all, a good herding dog knows when and what to herd. Unlike many herding

Aussie Rescue

Levi had one day left to live. With a life spent in kennel seclusion, Levi had finally given up on people, resorting to barking at them as they passed. His owner called him dangerous and gave him a death sentence. Sian, too, was not the dog her new family expected. With three children and working parents, little time was left for a rambunctious pup that only got wilder with age. Finally, the ultimatum: Sian had to go!

Levi and Sian were lucky. Levi was rescued by a new owner who worked with him to renew his faith in people. Sian eventually found a new owner who channeled her boundless energy into obedience, tracking, agility, and flyball. They rewarded their saviors with the kind of deep bond shared only in the closest relationships. They also shared their good fortune by helping others in different ways. Levi's dire situation, with no one to turn to for help, spurred his new owner to begin helping other Aussies in need, ultimately helping to form the Aussie Rescue and Placement Helpline (ARPH). Sian was placed through ARPH; she now spreads joy by visiting nursing homes, bringing comfort to people in need of unconditional love. Both Levi and Sian exemplify that there is nothing wrong with most Aussies that find themselves suddenly unwanted. In fact, there's a little more to both of their stories.

The very first AKC show in which Aussies could compete was filled with excitement over which dog would win the first AKC points available to an Aussie. Levi not only won the points, but went on to win Best of Breed, first in the Herding group, and then the supreme award—Best in Show! He continued his winning streak by becoming the first Aussie Best in Show winner in Canada, won several more Best in Shows and Specialties, and was ranked the #1 or #2 show Aussie in America for the next four years. Levi's real name is AKC/CKC/ASCA/SKC/IABCA CH Red Oak's All Jazzed Up.

Sian's keen mind, which had been so desperate for stimulation, found it in the most challenging obedience exercises. She won the supreme obedience trial award—High in Trial—not just once, but many times, in American Kennel Club, Canadian Kennel Club, United Kennel Club, and Australian Shepherd Club of America competitions. The wild pup that nobody could live with is now known as U-CD/Can OTCH Bohren's Sian ARPH Two Five Eight UD, NA, ASCA CDX, CGC, TDI.

The "ARPH Two Five Eight" of Sian's name signifies that she was the 258th Aussie placed through ARPH. The current ARPH Aussies awaiting placement have numbers in the thousands. Even more Aussies await adoption with yet other Aussie Rescue groups. Each one has the potential to be a great dog, whether it is a competition dog, stock dog, and most important of all, lifelong companion. All they need is a chance with the right person.

breeds, Aussies are not overly enthusiastic barkers. They will bark an alert if something seems amiss, and they may bark in play, but they do not (as a rule) bark incessantly unless they are bored and neglected. The key traits of the herding dogs are intelligence and energy. These are traits that seem good, but can be troublesome for pet owners.

Intelligence

The Aussie is uncannily intelligent. It has to be in order to learn and instantly respond to fairly complicated commands, as well as to think on its own in controlling stock. Most people think they want an intelligent dog, but very few people are prepared to deal with and nurture that intelligence. An intelligent child that is given no direction or stimulation is on its way to becoming a problem child; the same is true for an intelligent dog. If you plan to keep your dog in a cage a good part of the day, or even locked in the house alone while you work, then you don't want a dog whose mind is racing with ideas and a need for entertainment. You want a dull dog (actually, if you plan to ignore your dog you want a stuffed dog). An intelligent dog will look for ways to entertain itself and it will find them. It will dig, bark, get into the garbage, redecorate, escape, and come up with some amazingly mischievous ideas. Then what happens? Owners of such dogs try to remove all possible items the dog could entertain itself with, or lock the dog in a cage or run. The dog will always find a way to do something, even if it is only barking or biting itself—and when it finally gets a chance to do something, it is so crazed with relief that its owners consider it uncontrollable. They conclude that this supposedly intelligent breed is actually stupid and wild, and take it on a one-way trip to the dog pound. An intelligent dog needs intelligent things to do.

Energy Level

The Aussie is also a tireless athlete. Herding is not a short-term activity; the day of the working ranch dog is long and hard. The herding dog must be able to travel mile after mile, ever ready with short bursts of speed, hairpin turns, and skidding stops. Even when at a standstill it is ever vigilant, always on the alert for breaking stock, intruders, or its master's next command. Again, most people think they want an active dog, but far too often they place that active dog in a cage or apartment and think a walk around the neighborhood will satisfy its needs. It will not. The Aussie needs to run long and hard. If not given the chance to expend its large energy reserves, it will try to do so inside the house. Then its owners become more and more irritated with the dog, finally label it as hyperactive, and take it to the dog pound. An active dog needs activity.

Make sure you understand the Aussie before inviting one into your home. You are the one that can read and do research; your future Aussie doesn't have that advantage. It is at the mercy of its breeder's and future owner's good sense and judgment. Your Aussie is simply doing what it has been selected to do for uncounted generations.

OBTAINING AN AUSTRALIAN SHEPHERD

The Aussie's heritage as a dog bred primarily for working ability rather than looks has resulted in a breed with a wide variety of different but equally correct types. It has also led some people to erroneously adopt the Australian Shepherd name to refer to any generic herding dog; however, the Australian Shepherd is a distinct pure breed of dog. Authentic Aussies have several traits in common that are easy to discern as long as you know what to look for.

Finding an Aussie

Before embarking on your search for an Aussie, take a moment to clarify exactly what traits you feel are most important in your new dog. Most people insist upon good temperament, good health, and good looks. Some people also want promising herding, show, or obedience potential.

Good Temperament

More than owners of most breeds, Aussie owners list temperament as the top priority in selecting a breed. Most Aussies do have excellent temperaments, but you should still take some precautions when choosing your future partner.

"Can we go home with you?" As if you could really say no!

The personality of the sire and dam are the best indicators of that of their offspring. The Aussie is naturally wary of and reserved with strangers, but it should not act afraid or aggressive. A dam with very young puppies may act protectively; if so, she should be revisited when the pups are a little older.

The presence of obedience or herding titles in the pedigree indicates not only obedient ancestors, but breeders who care about temperament. Aussies are talented obedience and herding competitors, so it is not unusual to find a pedigree chock full of title holders. Note that a dog from a strong herding background may not be the best choice for a sedentary lifestyle (but then, no Aussie is); however, it is strongly desirable if you wish to work stock. Many true working Aussies have no titleholders in their backgrounds; they are too busy pursuing stock to take time off to pursue titles. Your best evidence is to watch the parents or other relatives actually working stock on the ranch.

Equally important is the environment in which the puppy is raised. Pups raised with minimal (or unpleasant) human contact during their critical period of development (from about six to ten weeks of age) may have some lifetime personality problems. Notice how the breeder interacts with the adults and pups, and whether the puppies are being raised underfoot (good) or out of sight (bad).

Good Health

Aussies are generally a healthy and hardy breed, commonly reaching the age of 12 or more. The chances of sharing a long life with your Aussie will be greatly increased if you carefully screen your source to ensure that your potential pup is as free as possible from hereditary problems. It may seem initially easier to run out and buy the first cute Aussie pup you find, but the effort you save will be inconsequential compared to the time, expense, and grief you will encounter if that pup later develops a serious hereditary illness. No matter how much research you do into the background of any puppy, there is no guarantee that your dog will live a long and healthy life, but why not go with the odds and choose a dog from the healthiest background possible?

Every pure breed of dog is a pure breed because it has only a subset of the genes available to the entire canine population. Sometimes this subset of genes includes genes responsible for a disease. When genes for a particular disease are more common in one breed than in another, that breed is said to have a hereditary predisposition to that disease. The Australian Shepherd has hereditary predispositions to several health problems, with the most common hereditary problems affecting the eyes.

Hereditary Eye Problems

Many of the collie-type breeds tend to share similar eye problems, suggesting a common ancestral basis originating before the time the breeds diverged, in some cases over 100 years ago; thus, these problems are not manifestations of current poor breeding, as is sometimes contended. In fact, significant progress has been made in decreasing the frequency of these disorders. Breeders now have weapons against these disorders that were unavailable to them in the past, and it is unconscionable for an Aussie breeder to fail to take precautions against hereditary eye disorders. The simplest safeguard is to breed only stock that has been cleared of any eye disorders by a licensed veterinary ophthalmologist. Most breeders will register their cleared dogs with the Canine Eye Registry Foundation (CERF) or, less commonly, the Institute for Genetic Disease Control in Animals (GDC). Note that the results of eye exams are typically valid for only one year; because many eye problems may not arise until later in life, breeding stock should be reexamined on a yearly basis. Note also that a clear exam is nonetheless no guarantee that the dog is not a carrier of a genetic disorder.

The following hereditary eye problems are the most prevalent in Australian Shepherds:

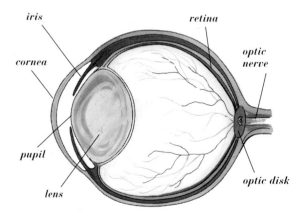

iris   *retina*

optic nerve

cornea

pupil

optic disk

lens

A normal dog's eye.

Cataracts: Opacities in the lens, called cataracts, block the light from reaching the retina. Although many dogs get cloudy lenses when they get old, hereditary cataracts tend to be more opaque and to occur in young dogs. Hereditary cataracts may show up in Aussies as young as 18 months of age.

Collie eye anomaly (CEA): In CEA, several structures in the rear portion of the eye develop abnormally. These include the retina (part of the eye containing the light-sensitive cells), retinal blood vessels, tapetum (the reflective layer responsible for "eyeshine" at night), and the optic disk (place where the nerve from the eye to the brain leaves the eye). CEA varies greatly in severity between affected dogs; mild cases can result in a large blind spot, and more severe cases can result in retinal detachment and blindness.

CEA can be detected in pups as young as six to eight weeks of age, but does not get worse with age. In fact, it sometimes appears to improve (a phenomenon known as "go normal"), although this appearance is caused by other parts of the maturing eye obscuring small affected areas. Any new Aussie pup should be examined by your veterinarian (or better, a veterinary ophthalmologist) as a condition of sale.

Colobomas: Colobomas refer to a failure of proper closure of fetal tissue, resulting in open pits in various structures of the eye. Colobomas of the retina or optic disk are often associated with CEA. Iris colobomas, which appear as openings in the colored portion of the eye, are more common in merle or predominantly white Aussies. Do not confuse iris colobomas with heterochromia, which is an iris of more than one color. Heterochromia is often seen in merles and is not considered a defect.

Aussie Sense: Vision

It is often assumed that herding dogs have superior vision to other dogs, but in fact, the question is still up in the air. The canine eye is superior to the human eye at seeing in very dim light. This ability comes in part from a reflective structure (the tapetum lucidum) in the back of the eye that reflects light back into the light sensitive cells of the retina, in essence, magnifying the light. The reflected light is the eyeshine you may see from your Aussie's eyes at night when you shine a light into them. The dog's ability to see in dim light is also in part due to the fact that it has a much greater proportion of the type of retinal cells (rods) that are highly sensitive to dim light than do humans.

The price the dog pays for this night vision is the sacrifice of keen detail and color vision. The dog's sense of color is like that of what is commonly called a "color-blind" person, which is not really blind to color at all. That is, they confuse similar shades of yellow-green, yellow, orange, and red, but can readily see and discriminate blue, indigo, and violet from all other colors and from each other.

Distichiasis: In distichiasis some of the eyelashes grow abnormally from the lids and contact the surface of the eye, constantly irritating it. Surgical removal is necessary.

Retinal dysplasia: Retinal dysplasia refers to abnormal development of the retina, which often leads to folds in the retina and detached retinas.

Progressive retinal atrophy (PRA): PRA is a condition in which the light-sensitive cells of the retina deteriorate. Although a few Aussies have been reported to have PRA, some speculation exists that these dogs may instead have had retinal problems due to trauma while working stock.

Other Hereditary Disorders

Canine hip dysplasia (CHD): The bane of many large breeds, in CHD the ball of the femur (thigh) bone does not fit properly in the socket of the pelvic bone. Although the condition is reported in Aussies, it is relatively uncommon compared to its frequency in other similarly sized breeds. Still, breeders should not become complacent. Hip radiographs (X rays) can be diagnostic of dysplasia before outward signs of the disorder can be perceived. Radiographs are rated by either the Orthopedic Foundation for Animals (OFA), the Pennsylvania Hip Improvement Program (PennHIP), or the GDC. Uninformed breeders may insist that their dogs have good hips because they are free of lameness or because of the way they sit or lie down, but these are naïve beliefs.

CHD has been shown to have a hereditary basis, but it is a complex disorder involving many factors. This means that it is possible that parents free of the condition can still produce dysplastic offspring, and dysplastic parents can produce clear offspring. On the whole, however, the chances are far greater of getting clear puppies from clear parents.

Epilepsy: Abnormal bursts of electrical impulses in the brain can result in seizures, which may include rigidity or jerking of the limbs, vocalizing, drooling, loss of consciousness, or a number of other symptoms. When repeated seizures occur without a detectable cause, the condition is termed epilepsy.

Nasal solar dermatitis ("Collie nose"): This condition is now considered to be a type of autoimmune condition called discoid lupus erythematosus (DLE), in which the body's own immune system turns against the cells of the outer nose. The nose loses its dark pigmentation, becomes reddened, scaly, crusted, and, eventually, ulcerated. Exposure to the sun worsens the condition. Although the hereditary nature is not understood, because it is more common in certain breeds (including Aussies and most collie types) it is assumed to have a genetic component. As in most autoimmune diseases, females are more often affected than males. Treatment is with a combination of sunscreens, anti-inflammatory drugs, and, in severe cases, drugs to suppress the immune system. Although it is reported in Aussies, it is nonetheless uncommon.

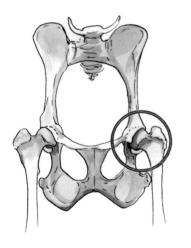

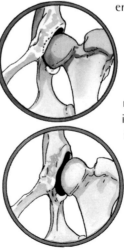

In hip dysplasia, the head of the femur does not fit snugly into the socket of the pelvis.

Black and tan with white trim.

Red merle with white trim.

Cleft palate syndrome: A rare sex-linked disorder found in Australian Shepherds, a cleft palate is the least of the problems affected dogs have. Affected males also have overwhelming skeletal abnormalities and die as a result of their problems; carrier females have minor skeletal abnormalities, such as extra toes.

von Willebrand's disease (vWD): Although not common, some Aussies are afflicted with vWD, a dominantly inherited bleeding disorder caused by a deficiency of clotting factor VIII. Symptoms include nosebleeds, hematomas (from bleeding under the skin), or occasional lameness caused by bleeding into the joints. Some other Aussies have been diagnosed with hemophilia, which is another type of bleeding disorder.

Pelger-Huet anomaly (PH): PH is an inherited developmental abnormality of one type of white blood cell. Dogs with only one copy of the gene for PH exhibit few, if any, clinical problems, although a practical problem can occur because many of the unusual blood findings can be mistaken for a severe bacterial infection or the early stages of leukemia. Further, if two dogs with PH are bred, they will likely produce some offspring with two copies

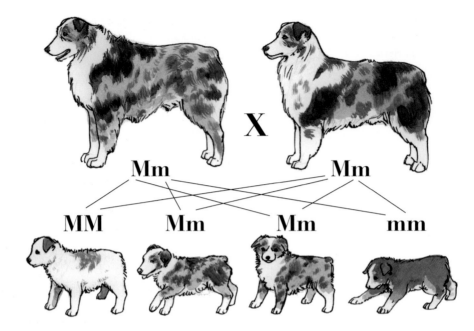

Mm X Mm

MM   Mm   Mm   mm

of the gene, which usually results in fetal death or severe skeletal deformities.

Patent ductus arteriosis (PDA): Part of the normal process of development is to close off the embryonic blood vessel connecting the pulmonary artery to the aorta around the time a puppy is born. In some Aussies this vessel persists into adulthood, causing the heart to pump blood less efficiently. It may be suspected in a young dog that tires easily or that has a heart murmur, but a definite diagnosis can be made by means of a heart ultrasound.

Thyroid disease: An increasing problem in many breeds is hypothyroidism, in which the thyroid gland is underactive. This results in a number of subtle signs, including lethargy, weight gain, and symmetrical hair loss. Diagnosis is made with a blood test.

A breeding of merle (Mm) to a merle (Mm) produces 50% merles (Mm), 25% non-merles (mm), and 25% lethal homozygous merles (MM).

Homozygous merle: Most people think of a merle-colored Aussie when they set out to find a puppy. They may naturally assume that the best way to get a merle puppy is to find a litter with two merle parents. Many inexperienced breeders also assume that the best way to get merles is to breed from two merle parents. This is a grave mistake.

The merle allele *(M)* is a dominant gene; only one copy of it is required in order to result in merle coloration. A dog with one copy of the *M* allele would be merle, and have the genotype *Mm* (so-called heterozygous merle). A dog with no *M* allele would not be merle, and would have the genotype *mm* (so-called homozygous non-merle.)The problem arises with a dog with two *M* alleles, having the genotype *MM* (so-called homozygous merle, or double merle.) The *M* allele is actually an incompletely dominant gene, because the presence of two *M* alleles does not result in merle, but instead in a predominantly white dog with spots of merle. Note that although most double merles are predominantly white, some double merles from lines that are naturally extremely dark may not appear to be markedly white compared to other Aussies, but have much more white than is typical for their line.

Certain types of white coat color, including that caused by the *MM* genotype, are associated with a multitude of defects in many animal species. This is because the *MM* genotype also affects the presence of some internal pigment that is normally present prenatally, and that is necessary to route developing nerve fibers to their proper destinations. Animals lacking this guiding pigment have auditory and visual systems with misdirected nerve fibers, resulting in complete or partial deafness or blindness. Other problems reported in canine *MM* individuals include autoimmune disorders, organ failures, and microphthalmia (abnormally small eyeballs). Double merles are usually euthanized at birth; however, many double merles live full lives.

Note: White trim, such as that on the feet, tail tip, face, and collar, should not be confused with the white of double merles. This white trim pattern (called Irish marking) is due to a separate recessive gene at an entirely different location, and has no detrimental effects.

Don't be scared off by what may appear to be a long list of problems. The typical Australian Shepherd is healthy and free of hereditary disease—but don't be oblivious to these problems either.

Puppy Health Checklist

Your prospective puppy should:
- ✔ have its first vaccinations and deworming.
- ✔ be outgoing and active; avoid a puppy that shows signs of fearfulness or aggressiveness. If a pup is apathetic or sleepy, it could be that it just ate, but it could also be a sign of sickness.
- ✔ be clean, with no missing hair, crusted or reddened skin, or signs of parasites. Eyes, ears, and nose should be free of discharge.
- ✔ have pink gums; pale gums may indicate anemia.
- ✔ have no indication of redness or irritation around the anus.
- ✔ not be coughing, sneezing, or vomiting.
- ✔ not be thin or pot-bellied.
- ✔ not be dehydrated, which can suggest repeated vomiting or diarrhea. Test for dehydration by picking up a fold of skin and releasing it. The skin should "pop" back into place.

Good Looks

You want your Aussie to look like an Aussie, which means it will need to have at the very least some of the more important Aussie characteristics. The Australian Shepherd is a medium-sized dog with a cobby, athletic build, slightly longer than tall. Its coat is of medium length and slightly coarse texture. It has a fairly broad head with a muzzle of approximately the same length as the backskull. Its ears are triangular, set on high, and fold forward. It usually has a bobtail. These traits are

Aussies come in a rainbow of colors, but be aware that predominantly white Aussies may have problems with vision, or especially hearing.

the entire family available. By examining the pedigree for conformation champions, you can also get an idea of how well your dog's ancestors conform to the official standards.

Custom Choices

Finally, the fun part—deciding what color, sex, and age Aussie is best suited for you. These choices are all just part of personal preferences; you really can't go wrong (with one exception: the double merle).

Colors

Aussies come in what seems to be an amazing array of colors, but the diversity can be explained by the interactions of four main color choices:

✔ black vs. liver
✔ merle vs. non-merle
✔ self vs. tan-pointed
✔ solid vs. white trimmed

Aussies can have either a black or brown (liver) base color. The black is due to a dominant allele *(B)*, and the brown is due to a recessive allele *(b)*. A dog with two *b* alleles will have no black pigment on its body, which means that the nose and eye rims (which are usually black in black Aussies), will be liver-colored. The eyes also tend to be lighter colored.

The inheritance of merle is described on page 18. Merles and non-merles are equally correct and equally healthy, although merles are prone to a few more minor eye problems. Phantom

the basics of Aussie type; more exacting requirements are set forth in the Australian Shepherd standard of perfection (see The ASCA Standard, pages 105–108).

Conformity to the official standards also requires sound body structure. Soundness refers to the ability to move in an efficient manner so that your Aussie can run, herd, and play tirelessly. Unsound Aussies may have feet that point outward rather than forward, or may have legs that interfere with each other when trotting, or may have any number of structural faults that result in an inefficient stride. Soundness is a trait more vital to the show or working dog than to the pet. Even some great working dogs are not particularly sound by show standards but are certainly proven by performance.

The appearance of the sire and dam of the litter is the best indication of the looks of their offspring. Good breeders will have photos of

Don't forget the adult Aussie who would love to share your life.

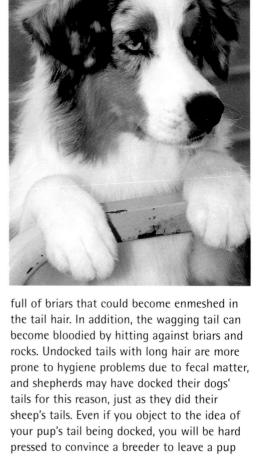

merles are merles with such small areas of dilute pigment that they may appear to be non-merles. Double merles result in Aussies that are predominantly white and that may be unhealthy. Do not get a predominantly white Aussie!

All colors and patterns can either be self (meaning distributed over all the dark areas of the body) or tan-pointed (also called copper trim), where the eyebrows, cheeks, and inner legs are tan. In addition, all colors and patterns can be either without any white or with Irish marking, in which the lower legs, tail tip, muzzle, and collar are white.

Tails

Adult Aussies traditionally have very short tails, but not all of them are born that way; some are "natural bobs" that require no docking. It might seem that a natural bob is preferable but some evidence exists that dogs with naturally short tails are more prone to congenital spinal defects. In fact, natural bobs should never be bred to each other because their offspring are more likely to have spinal defects. Puppies usually have their tails docked within the first few days of life, either by a tight ligature that prevents blood from circulating in the tail so that it dies and falls off, or by cutting it off. Either way, many breeders contend that little or no pain is involved. In fact, research has shown that some pain likely is involved, but the extent of it cannot be measured.

Why dock tails? The tradition may have arisen because the first Aussies worked in areas full of briars that could become enmeshed in the tail hair. In addition, the wagging tail can become bloodied by hitting against briars and rocks. Undocked tails with long hair are more prone to hygiene problems due to fecal matter, and shepherds may have docked their dogs' tails for this reason, just as they did their sheep's tails. Even if you object to the idea of your pup's tail being docked, you will be hard pressed to convince a breeder to leave a pup undocked for you. If you changed your mind about getting the pup it would be difficult to place, and docking the tail of an older dog is definitely painful. Note, however, that in several European countries docking is illegal, so that unless they are natural bobtails Aussies often have long tails.

Male or Female?

Aussie males are larger (20 to 23 inches [51 to 58 cm] at the shoulder and from 50 to 65 pounds [23 to 29 kg]) and have longer coats, heavier bones, and larger heads than females. Females are about 18 to 21 inches (46 to 53 cm) tall and from 35 to 50 pounds (16 to 23 kg). Males tend to be somewhat prouder and more territorial; the drawback is they don't always get along well with other males. Males are also apt to go off in search of females, and often think nothing of repeatedly lifting their leg on your furniture to mark your house as their territory. On the other hand, females come in estrus ("season" or "heat") twice a year; this lasts for three weeks, during which time you must keep your female away from amorous neighborhood males who consider your house a singles bar. You must also contend with her bloody discharge and possible attempts to elope with her suitors. The solution for both sexes is neutering (see page 60).

Puppy or Adult?

The easiest time for puppies to change homes is between eight and twelve weeks of age, but if you definitely want a competition-quality dog you may have to wait until the pup is five or six months old. An adult Aussie may need a longer adjustment period. No matter what the age, if the puppy has been properly socialized (that is, treated gently and exposed to a variety of situations, people, and dogs), your Aussie will soon blend into your family life and love you as though it's always owned you. If you want to work stock with your dog, then you will want it to be introduced to nonthreatening stock, such as ducks, at a young age.

Puppies are not for everyone. No one can deny that a puppy is cute and fun, but a puppy is much like a baby; you can't ever be too busy to walk, feed, supervise, or clean (and clean and clean). If you work away from home, have limited patience, or heirloom rugs, an older puppy or adult may be a better choice. Young Aussie pups are actually fairly obedient, but if you think an adult Aussie is active, you haven't seen anything until you've seen a youngster in action.

Breeders may have older retired dogs available that would relish the chance to live as a pampered pet. Several rescue groups are devoted to finding homes for Aussies in need of loving homes (see listings on page 109). In most cases their only crime was the misfortune of being placed with uninformed owners.

Quality

Dogs are generally graded as pet, competition or working, and breeding quality.

A pet-quality dog is one that has some trait that would prevent it from winning in conformation, herding, or perhaps obedience competition, but still has good health and temperament. Being a pet is the most important role a dog can fulfill, and pet quality should never be belittled.

Competition- or working-quality dogs should first of all be pet quality; that is, they should have good temperament and health. Those destined for the show ring should portray the attributes called for in the breed standard so that they could be expected to become conformation champions. Those destined for stock work should have a strong desire to herd—they should have the promise of becoming dependable helpers with stock. Many Aussies are able to compete successfully in herding, obedience, and conformation.

Breeding-quality dogs come from impeccable backgrounds, and are of even higher quality than are competition-quality dogs. Breeding quality means more than the ability to impregnate or conceive, but far too often these are the only criteria applied to prospective parents by owners unduly impressed by a registration certificate. It is difficult to pick a competition-quality puppy at an early age; it is impossible to pick a breeding-quality puppy.

The better quality you demand, the longer your search will take. A couple of months is a reasonable time to look for a pet puppy, a couple of years for a breeding-quality dog. Begin your search for a high-quality Aussie by seeing as many Aussies as possible, talking to Aussie breeders, attending Aussie competitions, joining an Aussie Internet newsgroup, and reading every available Aussie publication.

AKC or ASCA Registration

In most breeds the decision regarding registration is simple: AKC-registered versus not registered at all. In Aussies the decisions regarding registration are far more complex.

The reason traces back to the dispute over the Aussie's future as a show versus a working dog. When the AKC began registering Australian Shepherds, many concerned breeders declined to register their stock because they feared AKC recognition would encourage overbreeding or breeding for only cosmetic traits; thus, while some great Aussies are AKC-registered, many equally beautiful purebred Aussies are instead registered with the Australian Shepherd Club of America (ASCA). In fact, the ASCA is not only the traditional registering body for Aussies, but the largest, with over 70,000 Aussies registered.

Those Aussie breeders who have interest only in stockwork prefer to register their dogs with the International English Shepherd Registry (IESR), also known as the National Stock Dog Registry (NSDR).

If you are not particularly interested in breeding or competing with your Aussie, the registering body will not be of primary importance. If you wish to compete with your dog, however, bear in mind that to compete in AKC events a dog must be AKC-registered, and to compete in ASCA events a dog must be ASCA-registered. Many Aussies are registered with both AKC and ASCA.

Even if you have no intention of competing with your Aussie, the type of registry can be an important factor. If you want to use your Aussie to work stock, you would be better served to choose an Aussie from a strong herding background, such as those registered with the ASCA or NSDR. The downside is that such dogs may be even more energetic than dogs from nonworking backgrounds, and energetic dogs can be a handful unless you give them a job to do. If you want your Aussie to look like the one you saw winning at a dog show, your best bet is to get an AKC- or ASCA-registered dog from a show line.

Nonregistered dogs make great pets; however, they are not eligible for conformation competition, and may be eligible for other AKC or ASCA performance competitions only upon applying for a special type of registration allowing for limited types of competition.

A final note of caution: Registered puppies should come with a pedigree and either a litter registration certificate, individual registration certificate, or statement in writing clearly stating why such documents are not being supplied.

AUSTRALIAN SHEPHERDS AS HOUSE PETS

The Aussie has always expected to be a real member of the family, sharing family activities and, of course, the family home. In turn, Aussie owners expect their charges to act civilized, not using the antique furniture as a chewbone or the heirloom rugs as a bathroom.

Your Aussie now faces the transition from canine litter member to human family member. Every day will be full of novel experiences and new rules. Your pup is naturally inquisitive and will need you to guide it toward becoming a well-mannered member of the household.

Half the excitement of welcoming a new dog is preparing for the big homecoming. Puppy-proofing your home will be a lot easier if you do it before your new puppy is underfoot, undoing everything as fast as you can do it. Much of the fun comes from an Aussie accessory buying spree. The best sources for supplies are large pet stores, dog shows, and discount pet catalogs.

Home sweet home. Invite your Aussie into your house as a full-fledged family member, and you will be rewarded with a full-fledged loyal companion.

Accessories for Aussies

Consider the following supplies:

✔ Buckle collar: for wearing around the house; avoid leather, which can stain the coat. A wide, soft collar is more comfortable for the dog than a narrow stiff collar.

✔ Nylon choke or martingale collar: safer for walking on lead, never to be left on the dog!

✔ Leash: nylon, web, or leather—never chain. An adjustable show lead is good for puppies.

✔ Lightweight retractable leash: better for older adults; be sure not to drop the leash as it can retract toward the pup and frighten it.

✔ Stainless steel food and water bowls: avoid plastic, which can cause allergic reactions and retain germs.

✔ Cage: large enough for an adult Aussie to stand up in without having to lower its head. You may need to divide it so that the available space for a puppy is smaller (see page 27).

✔ Exercise pen: tall enough that an adult Aussie can't jump over, or preferably with a top (see page 28 for a description).

✔ Toys: fleece-type toys, ball, stuffed animals, stuffed socks, empty plastic milk or soda bottles. Make sure no parts of toys can be pulled off and swallowed.

✔ Chewbones: the equivalent of a teething ring for babies. Avoid rawhide.

✔ Anti-chew preparations, such as Bitter Apple: The unpleasant taste discourages pups from chewing on items sprayed with it.

✔ Baby gate(s): better than a shut door for placing parts of your home off-limits. Do not use the accordion-style gates, in which a dog can get its head stuck and be asphyxiated.

✔ Soft brush.

✔ Nail clippers: Guillotine type is easier to use.

✔ Poop scoop: Two-piece rake type is best for grass.

✔ Dog shampoo (see page 62 for choices).

✔ First aid kit (see page 73 for contents).

✔ Food: start with the same food the pup is currently eating.

✔ Dog bed: a round cushion is heavenly, but you can also use the bottom of a plastic cage, or simply use an entire cage.

Potential Killers

✔ drugs
✔ chocolate (especially baker's chocolate)
✔ rodent, snail, and insect baits
✔ antifreeze
✔ household cleaners
✔ paint thinner
✔ toilet fresheners
✔ nuts, bolts, pennies, which can dissolve in the stomach and cause zinc toxicity
✔ pins and needles, and anything in a sewing basket
✔ chicken bones or any bone that could be swallowed or could splinter
✔ sponges and sponge rubber balls
✔ any other small items that a pup could swallow, which can cause intestinal blockage

Safety Measures

Your puppy will naturally want to explore every nook and cranny of your house. Part of the pup's exploratory tools are its teeth, and any chewed items left in its wake are your fault, not your pup's—you are the one who should have known better—therefore, do not lash out at your pup. Give your pup a tap on the nose along with a firm *"No,"* and remove the item. If you come across one of your cherished items chewed to bits and feel compelled to lash out, go ahead— hit yourself in the head a few times for slipping up. It may teach you a lesson!

Any place your Aussie may wander must be Aussie-proofed. The first step is to do everything you would do to baby-proof your home. Get down at puppy level and see what dangers beckon. Avoid the following dangers.

✔ Puppies love to chew electrical cords in half, and even lick outlets. These can result in death from shock, severe burns, and loss of jaw and tongue tissue. They can also pull electrical appliances down on themselves by pulling on cords.

✔ Jumping up on an unstable object (such as a bookcase) could cause it to come crashing down, perhaps crushing the puppy.

✔ Do not allow the puppy near the edges of high decks, balconies, or staircases. Use baby gates, temporary plastic fencing, or chicken wire if needed in dangerous areas.

✔ Doors can be a hidden danger area. Everyone in your family must be made to understand the danger of slamming a door. Use doorstops to ensure that the wind does not blow doors suddenly shut or that the puppy does not go behind the door to play. Be especially cautious with swinging doors; a puppy may try to push one open, become caught, try to back out, and strangle. The pup may not see a clear glass door and could be injured running into it. Never close a garage door with a puppy darting about. Finally, doors leading to unfenced outdoor areas should be kept securely shut. A screen door is a vital safety feature.

Dangers also abound in the yard. Check for poisonous plants, bushes with sharp, broken branches at Aussie eye level, and trees with dead branches or heavy fruits in danger of falling. Aussies can charge around the yard at breakneck speed, so you must remove anything that a leg or foot could hit. If you have a pool, be aware that although dogs are natural swimmers, you should teach your dog how to get out of the pool.

Housing

Before bringing your puppy home you should decide what parts of your home will be off-limits. Make sure that every family member understands the rules, and that they understand that sneaking the puppy onto off-limit furniture, for example, is not doing the puppy any favor at all. Like all dogs, Aussies enjoy the comfort of your chairs and sofas, but if you don't want them on the furniture, keep them off from the beginning. Don't pick the pup up to sit on your lap; instead, sit on the floor with it. Never fling the pup off furniture, or use mousetraps on furniture surfaces; both practices are dangerous and a terrible idea unless you like emergency visits to the veterinarian. There are several more humane items (available through pet catalogs) that emit a loud tone when a dog jumps on furniture, but these should not be necessary if you train your young puppy gently and consistently from the beginning.

The Kennel

A secure kennel run can be a convenient asset. It should be at least 6 feet (1.8 m) high and preferably have a top. Dogs can get more exercise in a long, narrow run as opposed to a square run of equal area. It should also have both shade and shelter. Dirt flooring can become muddy and harbor germs, as well as encourage digging. Cement flooring is easier to clean but is expensive. The best compromise flooring is probably pea gravel, which is fairly easy to keep clean. Beware—too fine a texture may cling to the dog's coat. The run can provide a secure area for your Aussie when you are away from home, but is not a substitute for a yard or a home.

The Cage (or "Crate")

Many new dog owners are initially appalled at the idea of putting their pet in a cage as though it were some wild beast. At times, though, your Aussie pup can seem to be a wild beast, and a cage is one way to save your home from ruination and yourself from insanity. A cage can also provide a quiet haven for your youngster. Just as you hopefully find peace and security as you sink into your own bed at night, your pup needs a place that it can call its own, a place it can seek out whenever the need for rest and solitude arises. Used properly, your Aussie will come to think of its cage not as a way to keep itself in, but as a way to keep others out!

Don't expect your dog to stay in a cage all day, every day, while you are at work. Overuse of the cage is not only unfair, and even cruel, to the dog, but can also lead to behavior problems. An Aussie is an intelligent, active dog. To

lock it in a cage without stimulation can result in such frustration and anxiety that the dog can begin to resent the cage and act uncontrollably when out of the cage. A cage should be the canine equivalent of a toddler's crib. It is a place for naptime, a place where you can leave your pup without worry of it hurting itself or your home. It is not a place for punishment, nor is it a storage box for your dog when you're through playing with it. Rethink getting an Aussie (or any dog) if you plan for it to live in a cage.

Nonetheless, the cage has its place in training. Place the cage in a corner of a quiet room, but not too far from the rest of the family. Put the pup in the cage when it begins to fall asleep, and it will become accustomed to using it as its bed. Be sure to place a soft blanket in the bottom. Also, by taking the pup directly from the cage to the outdoors upon awakening, the cage

will be one of the handiest housebreaking aids at your disposal.

The X-pen

An exercise pen (or "X-pen") fulfills many of the same functions as a cage. X-pens are transportable wire folding "playpens" for dogs, typically about 4 feet by 4 feet (1.2 m × 1.2 m). X-pens are a reasonable solution when you must be away from home for a long time, because the pup can relieve itself on paper in one corner, sleep on a soft bed in the other, and frolic with its toys all over. It's like having a little yard inside the home. The X-pen also provides a safe time-out area when you just need some quiet time for yourself, but before leaving your pup in an X-pen, make sure that it cannot jump or climb out. Covers are available for incorrigible escapees. If you use an X-pen, cover the floor beneath it with thick plastic (an old shower curtain works well), and then add towels or washable rugs for traction and absorbency. Again, do not expect to stick your Aussie in an X-pen all day every day and still have a sane dog.

Fencing

The number one Aussie accessory and lifesaver is a securely fenced yard. In today's world of automobiles and suburbs, a loose dog is at best an unwelcome visitor and, more often, a dead dog. Aussies can be gifted jumpers, climbers, diggers, and wrigglers, and are often tempted by the greener grass on the other side of the fence. Running stray dogs, playing chil-

As appealing a picture as it may be, never get a puppy as a surprise gift or bring it home to the chaos of Christmas morning.

dren, racing bicycles, or just the call of the wild may prove irresistible to your dog.

Don't make the mistake many new owners make of testing their less-than-perfect fence to see if it just might work after all. Many dogs are actually inadvertently taught to be gifted escape artists by such situations. When the Aussie hops over the short fence, it has learned a very bad lesson. Even if the owner now adds an extension to raise the fence, the dog now has the jumping idea firmly implanted in its repertoire, and will likely test the new fence. If that one, too, can be jumped, the owner is in for a problem. If you want your Aussie to stay in the yard, make your yard escape-proof from the beginning. Adding progressive fixes only teaches your dog to escape little by little, just as you would gradually make things tougher if you were purposefully teaching your dog to find a way out.

Invisible fences have become a popular alternative to traditional fences, but they do have some shortcomings. Because they only work with a dog that is wearing a special shock collar that is activated by the buried boundary wire, they can't keep out stray dogs that aren't wearing such a collar, nor can they keep out unscrupulous dog-nappers. In addition, an excited, determined, or fast-moving Aussie can be over the boundary before it has a chance to stop, and then find itself blocked out of the yard. Nonetheless, most owners report good results with these fences.

Never tie your dog out. It is cruel and dumb and is the perfect recipe for creating an aggressive, neurotic, unhappy dog—plus, your

Aussie can choke to death, hurt its neck, or be attacked by strays.

Housebreaking

Aussies are easy to housebreak; still, most people have unrealistic expectations of their dog's ability to become housebroken, based in part upon friends boasting about their little genius that was housebroken at two weeks of age or something similarly ludicrous. No matter how wonderful and smart your Aussie is, it probably will not have full control over its elimination until it is around six months old, and may not be reliably housebroken until a year old. Be aware of the following blunders in housebreaking:

1. The number one housebreaking mistake made by most puppy owners is to give their puppies too much unsupervised freedom in the house. All canines have a natural desire to avoid soiling their denning area. The den area is considerably smaller than your entire house, however, and it will take some training before your pup extends the notion of den to your home.

You can use your dog's cage as its den, but if the cage is too large, the puppy may simply step away from the area it sleeps in and relieve itself at the other end of the cage. An overly large cage can be divided with a secure barrier until the puppy is larger or housebroken. Even so, your puppy may step just outside the door of the cage and eliminate there, because to the pup, that fulfills the natural requirement of not eliminating in the den. The puppy has failed to realize that it has just soiled *your* den, and the more the pup soils in a particular spot, the more it is likely to return to that same spot.

2. The second big mistake puppy owners make is to allow accidents to happen. Puppies have very weak control over their bowels, so if you don't take them to their elimination area often, they may not be able to avoid soiling. Puppies, like babies, have to eliminate a lot. You can't just stick them in a cage all day while you are at work and think you won't return home to a messy cage and messy pup. A rule of thumb is that a puppy can, at most, hold its bowels for as many hours as the pup is months old. This means that a three-month-old can hold itself for three hours. If the pup is forced to stay in a cage longer, so that it can't hold itself and has to soil the cage, you are setting the stage for a big problem. Once they get used to eliminating in their cage, they may continue.

Puppies tend to relieve themselves in areas that smell like urine. This is why it is so critical to never let the pup have an accident indoors;

if it does, clean and deodorize the spot thoroughly and block the pup's access to that area. Use a pet deodorizer cleaner, and never use one containing ammonia—ammonia is a component of urine, so using an ammonia cleaner is like posting a sign that says "Go here!"

If you cannot be with your puppy for an extended period, you may wish to leave it outside (only in good weather and with cover) so that it will not be forced to have an indoor accident. If this is not possible, you may have to paper-train your puppy. Place newspapers on the far side of the room (or X-pen), away from the puppy's bed or water bowl; near a door to the outside is best. Place the puppy on the papers as soon as it starts to relieve itself.

A better option is to use sod squares instead of newspapers. Place the sod on a plastic sheet, and when soiled, take it outside and hose it off or replace it. By using sod, you are training the pup to relieve itself on the same surface it should eventually use outside. Place the soiled squares outside in the area you want your dog to use.

Because dogs are creatures of habit, housebreaking is more a matter of prevention than correction. To avoid accidents, learn to predict when your puppy will have to relieve itself. Immediately after awakening, and soon after heavy drinking or playing, your puppy will urinate. You will probably have to carry a younger baby outside to get it to the toilet area on time. Right after eating, or if nervous, your puppy will have to defecate. Circling, whining, sniffing, and generally acting worried usually signal that defecation is imminent. Even if the puppy starts to relieve itself, quickly but calmly scoop the pup up and carry it outside (the surprise of being picked up will usually cause the puppy to stop in midstream, so to speak). You can also clap your hands or make a loud noise to startle the pup so that it stops. You can add a firm *"No,"* but yelling and swatting are actually detrimental. When the puppy does relieve itself in its outside toilet, remember to heap on the praise and let your Aussie pup know how pleased you are. Adding a food treat really gets the point across. Keep some in a jar near the door and always accompany your pup outside so that you can reward it.

3. The number three housebreaking mistake made by dog owners is overuse of punishment. Even if you catch your dog in the act, overly enthusiastic correction tends only to teach the dog not to relieve itself in your presence, even when outside. This is why you should reward with a tidbit when the pup does relieve itself outside. Punishment doesn't make clear what is desired behavior, but reward makes it clear very quickly. Punishing a dog for a mess it has made earlier is totally fruitless; it only succeeds in convincing the dog that every once in a while, for no apparent reason, you are apt to go insane and attack it. It is a perfect recipe for ruining a trusting relationship. That "guilty" look you may think your dog is exhibiting is really fear that you have once again lost your mind.

4. The number four housebreaking mistake owners make is to open the door and push the pup outside by itself. After five minutes, the pup is let back in and promptly relieves itself on the rug. Bad dog? No, bad owner. Chances are the pup spent its time outside trying to get back inside to its owner. Puppies do not like to be alone, and knowing you are on the other side of the door makes the outdoors unappealing. In bad weather, the pup probably huddled against the door so it didn't miss it when it was again opened. The solution? You must go outside with the pup every time. Don't take it for a walk, don't play with it, simply go with it to its relief area, say *"Hurry up"* (the most popular choice of command words), and be ready to praise and perhaps give a treat when the pup does its deed. Then you can go to its play area or back inside.

As soon as you are hopeful your precocious puppy is housebroken, it will take a giant step backward and convince you there is no link between its brain and bowels. If your previously housebroken adult Aussie soils the house, it could be due to a physical or emotional problem. A physical examination is warranted any time a formerly housebroken dog begins to soil the house. You and your veterinarian will need to consider the following possibilities:

✔ Older dogs may simply not have the bladder control that they had as youngsters; a doggy door is the best solution.

✔ Older spayed females may "dribble"; ask your veterinarian about drug therapies.

✔ Several small urine spots (especially if bloody or dark) may indicate a bladder infection, which can cause a dog to urinate frequently.

✔ Sometimes a housebroken dog will be forced to soil the house because of a bout of diarrhea, and afterwards will continue to soil in the same area. If this happens, restrict that area from the dog, deodorize the area with an enzymatic cleaner, and revert to basic housebreaking lessons.

✔ Male dogs may "lift their leg" inside the house as a means of marking it as theirs. Castration will often solve this problem as long as it is performed before the habit has become established; otherwise, diligent deodorizing and the use of some dog-deterring odorants (available at pet stores) may help.

Little ones make new friends easily.

✔ Submissive dogs, especially young females, may urinate upon greeting you; punishment only makes this "submissive urination" worse. For these dogs, be careful not to bend over or otherwise dominate the dog and to keep greetings calm. Submissive urination is usually outgrown as the dog gains more confidence.

✔ Some dogs defecate or urinate due to the stress of separation anxiety; you must treat the anxiety to cure the symptom. Dogs that mess their cage when left in it are usually suffering from separation anxiety or anxiety about being closed in a cage. Other telltale signs of anxiety-produced elimination are drooling, scratching, and escape-oriented behavior. You need to treat separation anxiety (see page 33) and start cage training again, placing the pup in it for a short period of time and working up gradually to longer times. Dogs that suffer from cage anxiety but not separation anxiety do better if left loose in a dog-proofed room.

Behavior Problems

No Aussie could really be awful, but even the best dogs with the best owners can sometimes do the worst things. Too often distraught owners get their training advice from the next-door neighbor or even dog trainers who don't have a scientific background in dog behavior analysis. Great strides have been made in recent years in canine behavioral therapy, so, if you're having a serious problem with your pet, before despairing, consult a certified canine behaviorist, who may employ a combination of conditioning and drug therapy to achieve a cure. Veterinarians can sometimes offer advice, but few are extensively trained in behavior. As a first step in any serious behavior problem, a thorough veterinary exam should be performed.

Sometimes the owner inadvertently makes the behavior worse, often through the overuse of punishment. If punishment doesn't work the first time, why do owners think that it will work the second, third, or fourth time? As the misbehavior continues in the face of punishment, the owners lay the blame on the dog. Inability to deal with what seems like inexcusable behavior too often leads the Aussie to the animal shelter.

Home Destruction

One of the most common canine behavior problems is home redecoration. Owners too often assume that the dog is angry at being left alone, and seeks to spite the owner by venting its rage on the home and its contents. Owners who continue to believe this erroneous idea never cure their dogs. Remember: Dogs never destroy out of spite.

Separation anxiety: The problem for many Aussies arises when their people leave them all alone. Being left alone is an extremely stressful situation for highly social animals. They react by becoming agitated and trying to escape from confinement. The telltale signature of a dog suffering from separation anxiety is that most of their destructive behavior is focused around doors and windows. Punishing the dog

When you play hard, you sleep hard.

is ineffective because it actually *increases* the anxiety level of the dog as it comes to both look forward to and dread its owner's return.

The proper therapy is treatment of the dog's fear of being left alone. This is done by leaving the dog alone for very short periods of time and gradually working up to longer periods, taking care to never allow the dog to become anxious during any session. When you *must* leave the dog for long periods during the conditioning program, leave it in a different part of the house than the one in which the conditioning sessions take place.

When you return home, refrain from a joyous reunion scene. No matter what the condition of the home, greet the dog calmly or even ignore it for a few minutes, to emphasize the point that being left was really no big deal. Then have the dog perform a simple trick or obedience exercise so that you have an excuse to praise it. It takes a lot of patience, and often a whole lot of self-control, but it's not fair to you or your dog to let this situation continue.

Frustration or boredom: Not all home destruction arises from separation anxiety. Puppies are natural demolition dogs. The best

cure (besides adulthood) is supervision. Adult Aussies still may destroy items through frustration or boredom. The best way to deal with these dogs is to provide both physical interaction (such as chasing a ball) and mental interaction (such as practicing a few simple obedience commands) an hour or so before leaving your dog. Several toys are available that can provide hours of entertainment.

Fearfulness

The cardinal rule of working with a fearful dog is to never push it into situations that might overwhelm it.

Although usually happy to meet new friends, the Aussie can be a bit cautious about strangers. Never force a dog that is afraid of people to be petted by somebody it doesn't know; it in no way helps the dog overcome its fear and is a good way for the stranger to get bitten. Strangers should be asked to ignore shy dogs, even when approached by the dog. Dogs seem to fear the attention of a stranger more than they fear the strangers themselves. When the dog gets braver, have the stranger offer it a tidbit, at first while not even looking at the dog. Gradual desensitization is time-consuming, but the best way to alleviate any fear.

Fear of thunder is a common problem in older dogs. Try to avoid it by acting cheerful when a thunderstorm strikes, and play with your dog or give it a tidbit. Once a dog develops a thunder phobia, try to find a recording of a thunderstorm, then play it at a very low level and reward your dog for calm behavior. Gradually increase the intensity and duration of the recording.

Never coddle your Aussie when it acts afraid, because it reinforces the behavior. It is always useful if your Aussie knows a few simple commands; performing these exercises correctly gives you a reason to praise the dog and also increases the dog's sense of security because it knows what is expected of it. For all causes of fear, the concept is the same: Never hurry, and never push the dog to the point that it is afraid.

Aggression

In some breeds aggression often results from a dog's attempts to dominate its owners. This is virtually never the case in Aussies. Some Aussies will herd other pets and children, but all Aussies can be taught not to do so. Many people erroneously believe that Aussies are being aggressive when they try to herd children, especially when nipping or grasping is involved, but this is more likely to be due to their herding instinct. Nonetheless, it can be unnerving. To dissuade an Aussie from acting in this manner, start young. True, it may seem cute in a puppy, but it will not be cute in an adult. First, try to prevent children from tempting the puppy with too much rambunctious behavior. If the dog does chase a child, the child should be instructed to stop, turn sideways to the dog with arms folded, and say *"No"* firmly. At the same time you can throw a can with some pennies in it (not *at* the dog!) so the rattling disrupts the dog's behavior, or give the dog a spritz of water from a water pistol.

Some dogs are afraid of children, either because they don't understand what they are or because they have had bad experiences with them. Introduce dogs and children to each other carefully, encouraging the child to be gentle and to offer the dog a treat. Unlike in humans, where direct eye contact is seen as a sign of sincerity, staring a dog directly in the eye is interpreted by the dog as a threat. It can cause a fearful dog to bite. Teach children not to stare at a strange dog.

Barking

The surest way to make your neighbors dislike your dog is to let it bark unchecked. Allow your Aussie to bark momentarily at strangers, and then call it to you and praise it for quiet behavior, distracting it with an obedience exercise if need be.

Isolated dogs will often bark through frustration or as a means of getting attention and alleviating loneliness. Even if the attention gained includes punishment, the dog will continue to bark in order to obtain the temporary presence of the owner. The simplest solution is to move the dog's quarters to a less isolated location. The distraction of a special chew toy, given only at bedtime, may help alleviate barking. In more stubborn cases, the use of collars that emit a whiff of citronella whenever the

Guidelines for Good Behavior

✔ Harsh corrections only make matters worse.
✔ Dogs live in the present and cannot make the connection between their earlier misdeeds and later punishment.
✔ Dogs repeat actions that bring immediate rewards.
✔ Dogs don't understand the concept of making an exception "just this once."
✔ Dogs hear what you say, not what you mean to say. Be consistent with commands.

dog barks have proved effective. The pup that must spend the day home alone is a greater challenge. Again, the simplest solution is to change the situation—a good excuse to get two Aussies!

Body language: (a) confident posture (yawning, panting, drooling, or slinking would indicate lack of confidence); (b) extremely submissive posture (ears back, body lowered, head averted); (c) dominant, aggressive posture (upright and stiff stance, direct stare, raised hackles); (d) playful posture (wagging rear end or tail, lowered front, opened mouth).

TRAINING AUSTRALIAN SHEPHERDS

Your Aussie will need some guidance in order to be a civilized member of society. You have an advantage, however—Aussies, especially young Aussies, are natural followers, not leaders. Your Aussie will elect you as its leader, and will expect you to guide. With the right methods, you will find that guiding your Aussie is both fun and easy.

Dog training methods have changed little through the years, but they should have. Old-fashioned dog training methods based on force are difficult, ineffective, and no fun for either dog or trainer. Punishment may tell a dog what not to do, but it can't tell a dog what it should do.

Remember that your role should be that of teacher, not drill master; your goal is to teach through guidance, not punishment.

Training Tips

Use the methods the professionals use, and you will be astounded by what your Aussie can learn.

1. Guide, don't force: Aussies already want to please you; your job is to simply show them the way. Forcing them can distract or intimidate them, actually slowing down learning.

A mind is a terrible thing to waste—especially one with the potential of a young Aussie.

2. Train before meals: Your Aussie will work better if its stomach is not full, and will be more responsive to food rewards. Never try to train a sleepy, tired, or hot dog.

3. Happy endings: Begin and end each training session with something the dog can do well. Keep sessions short and fun—no longer than 10 or 15 minutes. Dogs have short attention spans and you will notice that after about 15 minutes their performance will begin to suffer unless a lot of play is involved. To continue to train a tired or bored dog will result in the training of bad habits, resentment in the dog, and frustration for the trainer. Especially when training a young puppy, or when you only have one or two different exercises to practice, quit while you are ahead! Keep your Aussie wanting more, and you will have a happy, willing, obedient partner.

4. Once is enough: Repeating a command over and over, or shouting it louder and louder, never helped anyone, dog or human, understand what is expected of them. Your Aussie is not hard of hearing.

5. The best-laid plans: Finally, nothing will ever go just as perfectly as it seems to in all of the training instructions; however, although there may be setbacks, you *can* train your dog, as long as you remember to be consistent, firm, gentle, realistic, and, most of all, patient.

Aussie Sense: Hearing

Your Aussie can hear much higher frequencies than you can, and so can be irritated by high hums from your TV or from those ultrasonic flea collars. The high-pitched "dog whistles" so popular years ago emit a tone higher than humans can hear, but well within the dog's range. Dogs need to be trained to respond to these whistles just as they would any other command or signal. A problem is that owners can't tell when the whistle malfunctions.

Ultrasonic training devices now available emit a high-frequency sound inaudible to us but irritating and distracting to dogs. They can be a useful training aid for disrupting unwanted behavior, but only if accompanied by rewarding the dog for correct behavior.

Timing

The first ingredient in any command is your dog's name. You probably spend a good deal of your day talking, with very few words intended as commands for your dog, so warn your dog that this talk is directed toward it.

Many trainers make the mistake of simultaneously saying the command word *at the same time* that they are placing the dog into position. *This is incorrect.* The command comes immediately before the desired action or position. The crux of training is anticipation; the dog comes to anticipate that after hearing a command it will be induced to perform some action, and it will eventually perform this action without further assistance from you. On the other hand, when the command and action come at the same time, not only does the dog tend to pay more attention to your action of placing it in position, and less attention to the command

word, but the command word loses its predictive value for the dog. Remember: Name, command, action, reward! Don't forget to give your dog a release command such as *"OK!"* to tell it that it is free to go when you're through.

Rewards

Many years ago the idea was perpetuated that dogs should never be trained with food, yet professional animal trainers and animal learning scientists all knew that food training produced excellent results. Only recently has food-motivated training become accepted in training the family dog, and owners are finding dogs that learn faster, mind more reliably, work more eagerly, and have a more trusting dog-owner relationship.

Praise can become a stronger motivator by always praising immediately before a food reward is given. In this way praise becomes a secondary reinforcer. Eventually, the dog can be weaned from the food and will come to work in large part for praise, but food should still be given as reward intermittently.

Food is used initially to guide the dog into position, and then to reward the dog when it is in place. After the dog knows what is expected, the food is held out of sight and only given to the dog when it has performed correctly. Ultimately, the dog is weaned from getting a food reward each time, but still gets one every once in a while. Such a randomized schedule has been shown to be effective in animals and humans.

Professional dog trainers go one step farther. They use a signal (such as that from a clicker) to instantly tell the dog when it has performed correctly. The signal is then followed by a food reward. A clicker signal is used because it is fast, noticeable, and something the dog otherwise does not encounter. In order to apply this technique to the following instructions, whenever giving a treat is mentioned, you should precede it with a clicker signal.

Training Equipment

Equipment for training should include a 6-foot (1.8-m) and a 20-foot (6-m) lightweight lead. For puppies it is convenient to use one of the lightweight adjustable-size show leads. Most Aussies can be trained with a buckle collar, but a nylon choke collar is also an acceptable choice as long as you know how to use it correctly.

A choke collar is not for choking! In fact, it is more correctly termed a slip collar. The proper way to administer a correction with a choke collar is with a *very* gentle snap, then immediate release. The choke collar is placed on the dog so that the ring with the lead attached comes up around the left side of the dog's neck, and through the other ring. If put on backwards, it will not release itself after being tightened (since you will be on the right side of your dog for most training). The choke collar should *never* be left on your Aussie after training sessions; there are too many tragic cases in which a choke collar really did earn its name after being snagged on a fence, bush, or even a playmate's tooth.

Basic Obedience

It's never too early or too late to start the education of your Aussie. With a very young Aussie, train for even shorter time periods. By the time your Aussie pup (here named

"Stinky") reaches six months, he should be familiar with the following commands:

"Watch Me"

A common problem when training any dog is that the dog's attention is elsewhere. You can teach your dog to pay attention to you by teaching it the *"Watch me"* command. Say *"Stinky, watch me,"* and when he looks in your direction, give him a treat or other reward. Gradually require him to look at you for longer and longer periods before rewarding him. Teach *"Watch me"* before going on to the other commands.

Tip: Teach stationary exercises on a raised surface. This allows you to have eye contact with your dog and gives you a better vantage from which to help your dog learn.

"Sit"

The easiest way to teach the *sit* is to stand in front of your pup and hold a tidbit above his eye level. Say *"Stinky, sit,"* and then move the tidbit toward your pup until it is slightly behind and above his eyes. You may have to keep a hand on

Correct placement of the choke collar.

his rump to prevent him from jumping up. When the puppy begins to look up and bend his hind legs, praise, then offer the tidbit. Repeat this, requiring the dog to bend his legs more and more until he must be sitting before receiving praise.

Tip: If your dog backs up instead of sits down, place his rear against a wall while training.

"Stay"

Teach your dog to sit and stay until given the release signal before walking through the front door or exiting your car.

Have your dog sit, then say "*Stay*" in a soothing voice (for commands in which the dog is not supposed to move, don't precede the command with the dog's name). If your Aussie attempts to get up or lie down, gently but instantly place it back into position. Work up to a few seconds, give a release word (*"OK!"*) and praise and give a tidbit. Next, step out (starting with your right foot) and turn to stand directly in front of your dog while it stays. Work up to longer times, but

don't ask a young puppy to stay longer than 30 seconds; the object is not to push your dog to the limit, but to let it succeed. You must increase your times and distances in very small increments. Finally, practice with the dog on lead by the front door or in the car.

Tip: Don't stare at your dog during the *stay*, as this is perceived by the dog as a threat and often intimidates it.

"Come"

Coming on command could save your dog's life. You want your puppy to respond to *"Stinky, come"* with the same enthusiasm as though you were setting down his supper; in other words, *"Come"* should always be associated with good things.

Think about what excites your Aussie and makes it run to you. For most young Aussies, the opportunity to chase after you is one of the grandest games ever invented—and of course, most young Aussies will jump at the chance to gobble up a special treat. Combine these two urges and use them to entice your Aussie to come on the run.

The best time to start is when your Aussie is a young puppy, but it is never too late. You will need a helper and an enclosed area; a hallway is perfect for a very young pup. Have your helper gently restrain the puppy while you back away and entice the puppy. Do whatever it takes at first. The point is to get the pup's attention, and to get him struggling to get away and get to you. Only at this point should you call out *"Stinky, come!"* with great enthusiasm, at the same time turning around and running away. Your helper will release the pup

Training to sit using treats.

at the same time, and you should let him catch up to you. Reward him by playing for a second, then kneel down and give him the special treat. Repeat this several times a day, gradually increasing the distance, taking care never to practice past the time when your pup begins to tire of the game.

Once your puppy has learned the meaning of *"Come,"* move your training outdoors. With the pup on lead, command *"Stinky, come!"* enthusiastically, and quickly run away. When he reaches you, praise and reward. If he ignores you for more than a second, tug on the lead to get the pup's attention, but do not drag him. Response to the *come* command is not one that can be put off until your dog feels like

No matter how much you trust your dog, use a long line when practicing around distractions.

coming. In addition, the longer you separate the tug from the command, the harder it will be for your pup to relate the two and, in the long run, the harder the training will be on the youngster. After the tug, be sure to run backwards and make the pup think that it was all part of the grand game.

Next, attach a longer line to the pup, allow him to meander about, and in the midst of his investigations, call, run backwards, and reward. After a few repetitions, drop the long line, let Stinky mosey around a bit, then call. If he begins to come, run away and let him chase you as part of the game. If he doesn't come, pick up the line and give a tug, then run away as usual. If at any time your Aussie runs the other way, never chase him—chase the line, not the dog. The only game an Aussie likes more than chasing you is being chased by you. It will always win. Chase the line, grab it, give it a tug, then run the other way.

As your dog becomes more reliable, you should begin to practice (still on the long line) in the presence of such distractions as other leashed dogs, unfamiliar people, cats or other animals, and cars. In most of these cases you should not let the dog drag the line, but hold on just in case the distractions prove too enticing.

Some dogs develop a habit of dancing around just out of reach of you, considering your futile grabs to be another part of this wonderful game. You can prevent this by requiring your dog to allow you to hold it by the collar before you reward it. Eventually, you may add sitting in front of you as part of the game.

Tip: Never have your dog come to you and then scold it for something it has done. In the dog's mind it is being scolded for coming, not for any earlier misdeed. Nor should you call your dog to you at the end of an off-lead walk. You don't want the dog to associate coming to you with relinquishing its freedom. Call it to you several times during the walk, reward it, and praise it, and then send it back out to play.

"Down"

When you need your Aussie to stay in one place for a long time, it is best for it to be left in a *down/stay*. Begin teaching the *down* command with the dog in the sitting position. Command *"Stinky, down,"* then show him a tidbit and move it below his nose toward the ground. If he reaches down to get it, give it to him. Repeat, requiring him to reach farther down (without lifting his rear from the ground) until he has to lower his elbows to the ground. Never try to force your dog into the *down* position, which can scare a submissive dog and cause a dominant dog to resist. Practice the *down/stay* just as you did the *sit/stay*.

Tip: Aussies don't mind learning the *down*, but some mind having to lie on a hard floor. Your initial training will be much easier if you do it on a soft warm surface.

"Heel"

Walking alongside you on lead may be a new experience for a youngster, and many will freeze in their tracks once they discover their freedom is being violated. In this case do not simply drag the pup along, but coax it with food. When the puppy follows you, praise and reward. In this way the pup comes to realize that following you while walking on lead pays off.

Some Aussies have a tendency to forge ahead, pulling their hapless owners behind them. Although at times this may be acceptable to you, at other times it will be annoying and perhaps even dangerous. After all, Aussies are strong! Even if you have no intention of teaching a perfect competition *heel*, you need to teach the *heel* as a way of letting your Aussie know it is your turn to be the leader.

Have your Aussie sit in *heel* position; that is, on your left side with its neck next to and parallel with your leg. Say *"Stinky, heel,"* and step off with your left foot first (remember that you stepped off on your right foot when you left your dog on a *stay*; if you are consistent, the foot that moves first will provide an eye-level cue for your dog). During your first few practice sessions you will keep him on a short lead, holding him in *heel* position, and of course praising him. The traditional method of letting the dog lunge to the end of the lead and then snapping it back is unfair if you haven't shown the dog what is expected of him at first. Instead, after a few sessions of showing your dog the *heel* position, give him a little more loose lead and use a tidbit to guide him into correct position. If your Aussie still forges ahead after you have shown it what is expected, pull it back to position with a quick gentle tug, then release, of the lead. If, after a few days practice, your dog still seems oblivious to your efforts, then turn unexpectedly several times; teach your dog that it is its responsibility to keep an eye on you. Keep in mind that every time you do this you cause your Aussie to heel a little bit farther back in relation to you, and that in the long run, more dogs have a problem with lagging way behind than with forging ahead. In other words, don't go overboard when trying to correct forging. It will tend to self-correct with just a little guidance.

As you progress you will want to add some right, left, and about-faces, and walk at all different speeds. Then practice in different areas (still always on lead) and around different distractions. You can teach your Aussie to sit every time you stop. Vary your routine to combat boredom, and keep training sessions short. Be sure to give the *"OK"* command before allowing your dog to sniff, forge, and meander on lead.

Tip: Keep up a pace that requires your Aussie to walk fairly briskly; too slow a pace gives your dog time to sniff, look all around, and in general become distracted; a brisk pace will focus the dog's attention upon you and generally aid training.

Canine Good Citizen Test

In order to formally recognize dogs that behave in public, the AKC offers the Canine Good Citizen (CGC) certificate, which requires your Aussie to

✔ accept a friendly stranger who greets you.

✔ sit politely for petting by a stranger.

✔ allow a stranger to pet and groom it.

✔ walk politely on a loose lead.

✔ walk through a crowd on a lead.

✔ sit and lie down on command and stay in place while on a 20-foot (6-m) line.

✔ calm down after play.

✔ react politely to another dog. React calmly to distractions.

✔ remain calm when tied for three minutes in the owner's absence, under supervision by a stranger.

Training to come using treats.

FEEDING YOUR AUSTRALIAN SHEPHERD

The Aussie's athletic build, as well as its condition, health, and ultimate longevity depend in part upon what food you choose to set in front of it—and all it takes is one dizzying trip through the dog food section of a supermarket, pet supply store, or dog show vendor aisle to leave you utterly baffled and feeling like the worst dog owner ever created. Before you become paralyzed with indecision, keep in mind that dog nutritionists have done most of the work for you, and that as long as your food passes some basic guidelines it will be adequate to sustain your dog's life. It may not make it bloom with condition, however. For that, you do need to do a little investigating on your own.

Feeding Basics

Although dogs are members of the order Carnivora (meat-eaters), they are actually omnivorous, meaning their nutritional needs can best be met by a diet derived from both animals and plants. Most dogs do have a decided preference for meat over non-meat foods, but a balanced meal will combine both meat and plant-based nutrients. These nutrients are commercially available in several forms. Most Aussie owners feed a combination of dry and canned food, supplemented with dog biscuits and possibly soft moist food.

✔ *Dry food* (containing about 10 percent moisture) is the most popular, economical, and healthy, but least enticing, form of dog food.

✔ *Semimoist foods* (with about 30 percent moisture) contain high levels of sugar used as preservatives. They are tasty, convenient, and very handy for traveling, but are not an optimal nutritional choice as a regular diet. Pay no attention to their meatlike shapes; they all start out as a powder and are formed to look like meat chunks or ground beef.

✔ *Canned foods* have a high moisture content (about 75 percent), which helps to make them tasty, but it also makes them comparatively expensive, since you are in essence buying water. A steady diet of canned food would not provide the chewing necessary to maintain dental health. In addition, a high meat content tends to increase levels of dental plaque.

Dog biscuits and carrots can help provide the chewing action necessary to get rid of some (but not all) dental plaque. The better varieties of dog biscuits provide complete

Good nutrition shows.

nutrition. They are most commonly used as snacks or treats.

The Association of American Feed Control Officials (AAFCO) has recommended minimal nutrient levels for dogs based on controlled feeding studies. Unless you are a nutritionist, the chance of your cooking up a homemade diet that meets these exacting standards is remote; therefore, the first rule is to select a food that states on the label that it not only meets the requirements set by the AAFCO, but also has been tested in *feeding trials.*

Feed a high-quality food from a name-brand company. Avoid food that has been sitting on the shelf for long periods, or that has holes in the bag or grease that has seeped through the bag. Always strive to buy and use only the fresh-est food available. Dry food loses nutrients as it sits, and the fat content can become rancid.

Shop around for a food that your Aussie enjoys. Mealtime is a highlight of a dog's day; although a dog will eventually eat even the most unsavory of dog foods if given no choice, it hardly seems fair to deprive your family member of one of life's simple, and for a dog, most important, pleasures. But beware: Dogs will often seem to prefer a new food when first offered, but this may simply be due to its novelty. Only after you buy a cupboard full of this alleged Aussie ambrosia will you discover it was just a passing fancy.

"He Ate What?"

Dogs can eat a variety of strange things. Some dogs have abnormal desires to ingest nonedible substances, including wood, fabric, or soil. Talk to your veterinarian about possible health problems that could contribute to these specific hungers, and about possible problems that could result from eating these items. The most common and seemingly appalling non-food item eaten by dogs is their own feces. This habit, called coprophagia, has been blamed on boredom, stress, hunger, poor nutrition, and excessively rich nutrition, but none of these has proved a completely satisfactory explanation. Food additives are available that make the stool less savory, and you can also try adding hot pepper to it, but a determined dog will not be deterred and the best cure is immediate removal of all feces. Many puppies experiment with stool-eating but grow out of it.

Aussie Sense: Taste

Dogs have most of the same taste receptors that we do, including similar sugar receptors (which explains why many have a sweet tooth), but their perception of artificial sweeteners is not like ours, and they seem to taste bitter to them. Research has shown that dogs in general prefer meat, of course, and while there are many individual differences, the average dog prefers beef, pork, lamb, chicken, and horsemeat, in that order.

Nutrition Basics

When comparing food labels, keep in mind that differences in moisture content make it difficult to make direct comparisons between the guaranteed analyses in different forms of food unless you first do some calculations to equate the percentage of dry matter food. The components that vary most from one brand to another are protein and fat percentages.

Protein provides the necessary building blocks for growth and maintenance of bones, muscle, and coat, and in the production of infection-fighting antibodies. The quality of protein is as important as the quantity of protein. Meat-derived protein is more highly digestible than plant-derived protein, and is of higher quality. Most Aussies will do fine on regular adult foods having protein levels of about 20 percent (dry food percentage).

Fat is the calorie-rich component of foods, and most dogs prefer the taste of foods with higher fat content. Fat is necessary to good health, aiding in the transport of important vitamins and providing energy. Dogs deficient in fat often have sparse, dry coats.

Choose a food that has a protein and fat content best suited for your dog's life stage, adjusting for any weight or health problems (prescription diets formulated for specific health problems are available). Puppies and adolescents need particularly high protein and somewhat higher fat levels in their diets, such as the levels found in puppy foods. Stressed, highly active, or underweight dogs should be fed higher protein levels or even puppy food. Obese dogs or dogs with heart problems should be fed a lower fat food. Older dogs, especially those with kidney problems, should be fed moderate levels of very high-quality protein. Studies have shown that high-protein diets do not cause kidney failure in older dogs, but, given a dog in which kidney stress or decompensation exists, a high-protein diet will do a lot of harm.

As important as the guaranteed analysis is the list of ingredients: A good rule of thumb is that three or four of the first six

Never Feed

- ✔ Chicken, pork, lamb, or fish bones. These can be swallowed and their sharp ends can pierce the stomach or intestinal walls.
- ✔ Any bone that could be swallowed whole. This could cause choking or intestinal blockage.
- ✔ Any cooked bone. Cooked bones tend to break and splinter.
- ✔ Mineral supplements unless advised to do so by your veterinarian.
- ✔ Chocolate. It contains theobromine, which is poisonous to dogs.
- ✔ Alcohol.

ingredients should be animal-derived. These tend to be tastier and more highly digestible than plant-based ingredients; more highly digestible foods generally mean less stool volume and fewer gas problems.

You may have to do a little experimenting to find just the right food, but a word of warning:

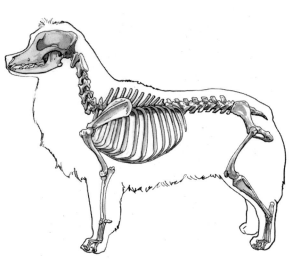

A strong skeleton comes from a balanced diet.

"What's for supper?"

One of the great mysteries of life is why a species, such as the dog, that is renowned for its lead stomach and preference to eat out of garbage cans, can at the same time develop violently upset stomachs simply from changing from one high-quality dog food to another—but it happens. So when changing foods you should do so gradually, mixing in progressively more and more of the new food each day for several days.

Avoiding Fat

The dog's wild ancestor, the wolf, evolved to survive feast and famine, gorging following a kill, but then perhaps waiting several days before another feast. In today's world, dogs can feast daily, and without the period of famine they can easily become obese.

An Aussie in proper weight should have an hourglass figure whether viewed from above or the side. There should be no roll of fat over the withers or rump. The stomach should be slightly tucked up. The ribs should be easily felt through a layer of muscle. The Aussie is an athlete, and should have an athlete's body: lean and muscular.

Overweight Aussies should be fed a high-fiber, low-fat, and medium-protein diet dog food. Such commercially available diet foods, which supply about 15 percent fewer calories per pound, are preferable to the alternative of just feeding less of a fattening food.

Aussies know how to get what they want and their owners usually oblige, but sometimes you have to practice tough love and say "no more food!"

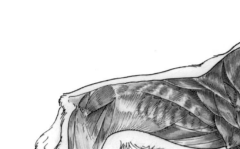

Good nutrition is essential to keep your Aussie's physique at its peak.

Many people find that one of the many pleasures of dog ownership is sharing a special treat with their pet. Rather than giving up this bonding activity, substitute a low-calorie alternative such as rice cakes or carrots. Make sure family members aren't sneaking the dog forbidden tidbits. Keep the dog out of the kitchen or dining area at food preparation or meal times. Schedule a walk immediately following your dinner to get your dog's mind off your leftovers—it will be good for both of you.

If your dog remains overweight, seek your veterinarian's opinion. Heart disease and some endocrine disorders, such as hypothyroidism or Cushing's disease, or the early stages of diabetes, can cause the appearance of obesity and should be ruled out or treated. However, as in humans, most cases of obesity are simply from eating more calories than are expended. Obesity predisposes dogs to joint injuries and heart problems. An obese Aussie cannot enjoy one of its greatest pleasures in life—the ability to run, jump, and frisk with boundless energy.

Underweight Aussies may gain weight with puppy food; add water, milk, bouillon, or canned food and heat slightly to increase aroma and palatability. Milk will cause many dogs to have diarrhea, so try only a little bit at first. Try a couple of dog food brands, but if your Aussie still won't eat, you may have to employ some tough love. Many picky eaters are created when their owners begin to spice up their food with especially tasty treats. The dog then refuses to eat unless the preferred treat is offered, and finally learns that if it refuses even that proffered treat, another even tastier enticement will be offered. Give your dog a good, tasty meal, but don't succumb to Aussie blackmail or you may be a slave to your dog's gastronomical whims for years to come.

Your veterinarian should examine your dog if its appetite fails to pick up, or if it simply can't gain weight. Even more worrisome would be a dog that suddenly loses its appetite or weight. Such a problem can be a warning sign of a physical disorder.

A sick or recuperating dog may have to be coaxed into eating. Cat food or meat baby food are both relished by dogs and may entice a dog without an appetite to eat.

Feeding Schedules

Very young puppies should be fed three or four times a day, on a regular schedule. Feed them as much as they care to eat in about

Some Common Dog Food Ingredients

✔ Meat: mammal flesh including muscle, skin, heart, esophagus and tongue
✔ Meat by-products: cleaned mammal organs including kidneys, stomach, intestines, brain, spleen, lungs, and liver, plus blood, bone, and fatty tissue
✔ Meat and bone meal: product rendered from processed meat and meat products, not including blood
✔ Poultry by-products: cleaned poultry organs, plus feet and heads
✔ Poultry by-products meal: product rendered from processed poultry by-products
✔ Fish meal: dried ground fish
✔ Beef tallow: fat
✔ Soybean meal: by-product of soybean oil

✔ Corn meal: ground entire corn kernels
✔ Corn gluten meal: dried residue after the removal of bran, germ, and starch from corn
✔ Brewer's rice: fragmented rice kernels separated from milled rice
✔ Cereal food fines: small particles of human breakfast cereals
✔ Beet pulp: dried residue from sugar beets, added for fiber
✔ Peanut hulls: ground peanut shells, added for fiber
✔ BHA, BHT, ethoxyquin, sodium nitrate, tocopherols (vitamins C and E): preservatives; of these, the tocopherols are generally considered to have the least health risks but also have the shortest shelf life

15 minutes. From the age of three to six months, pups should be fed three times daily, and after that, twice daily. Adult dogs can be fed once a day, but it is actually preferable to feed smaller meals twice a day.

Some people let the dog decide when to eat by leaving food available at all times. If you choose to let the dog "self-feed," monitor its weight to be sure it is not overindulging. Leave only dry food down; canned food spoils rapidly and becomes both unsavory and unhealthy. If your dog overindulges, you will have to intervene before you have a roly-poly Aussie on your hands.

Water

Water is essential for your Aussie's health and comfort. Don't just keep your dog's water bowl full by topping it up every day. Such a habit allows algae to form along the sides of the bowl, and gives bacteria a chance to multiply. Empty, scrub, and refill the water bowl daily. If the water bowl runs dry, your Aussie may turn to the toilet bowl as an alternative source; in fact, you should make it a practice to keep the lid down, because many dogs view the toilet bowl as an especially deluxe watering hole! It should go without saying that drinking from the toilet is not a healthy practice.

PREVENTIVE HEALTH CARE

An ounce of prevention really is worth a pound of cure. Preventive medicine encompasses accident prevention, vaccinations, and parasite control, as well as good hygiene and grooming. It is a team effort directed by your veterinarian but undertaken by you. Choose your veterinarian carefully, and take your duties seriously.

Health Checks

The only way you will know if your Aussie may be sick is to become intimately in tune with it when it's well. Take five minutes weekly to perform a simple health check, examining:

✔ the mouth for red, bleeding, swollen, or pale gums, loose teeth, ulcers of the tongue or gums, or bad breath
✔ the eyes for discharge, cloudiness, or discolored "whites"
✔ the ears for foul odor, redness, or discharge
✔ the nose for thickened or colored discharge
✔ the skin for parasites, hair loss, crusts, red spots, or lumps
✔ the feet for cuts, abrasions, split nails, bumps, or misaligned toes

Observe your dog for signs of lameness or incoordination, sore neck, circling, loss of muscle, and for any behavioral change. Run your

An ounce of prevention is worth a pound of cure—especially when it comes to dogs.

hands over the muscles and bones and check that they are symmetrical from one side to the other. Weigh your dog and observe whether it is putting on fat or wasting away. Check for any growths or swellings, which could indicate cancer or a number of less serious problems. A sore that does not heal or any pigmented lump that begins to grow or bleed should be checked by a veterinarian immediately. Look out for mammary masses, changes in testicle size, discharge from the vulva or penis, increased or decreased urination, foul-smelling or strangely colored urine, incontinence, swollen abdomen, black or bloody stool, change in appetite or water consumption, difficulty breathing, lethargy, gagging, or loss of balance.

Taking the Temperature

To take your dog's temperature, lubricate a rectal thermometer (preferably the digital type), insert it about 2 inches (5 cm) into the dog's anus, and leave it for about one minute. Do not allow your dog to sit down on the thermometer! Normal temperature for an Aussie is around 101°F (38°C), ranging from 100 to 102.5°F (37.8 to 39°C). Call your veterinarian immediately if the temperature is over 104°F (40°C).

Pulse

A good place to check the pulse is on the femoral artery, located inside the rear leg, where the thigh meets the abdomen. Normal pulse rates range from 80 to 140 beats per minute in an awake Aussie, and are strong and fairly regular.

External Parasites

Your Aussie's skin is its largest single organ, and the one most accessible to you. It is a major interface between your dog and the environment, and as such is vulnerable to a plethora of problems, many caused by fleas and ticks. Fleas can carry tapeworms, and ticks can carry Rocky Mountain spotted fever, tick paralysis, Lyme disease, babesiosis, and most commonly "tick fever" (erlichiosis)—all very serious diseases.

Ticks

Ticks can be found anywhere on the dog, but most often burrow around the ears, neck, chest, and between the toes. To remove a tick, use a tissue or tweezers, since some diseases can be transmitted to humans. Grasp the tick as close to the skin as possible, and pull slowly and steadily, trying not to leave the head in the dog. Clean the site with alcohol. Often, a bump will remain after the tick is removed, even if you got the head. It will go away with

Aussie Sense: Pain

Many Aussies can be amazingly stoic, even when they must be in pain. Because a dog may not be able to express that it is in pain, you must be alert to changes in your Aussie's demeanor. A stiff gait, low head carriage, reluctance to get up, irritability, dilated pupils, whining, or limping are all indications that your pet is in pain.

time. *Don't ever try to burn a tick out!* You may catch your dog on fire.

Fleas

Recent advances in flea control have finally put dog owners on the winning side. In any but the mildest of infestations, these new products are well worth their initial higher purchase price. Consider carefully the correct choice of products for your dog and situation:

✔ imidacloprid (such as Advantage) is a liquid applied once a month on the animal's back. It gradually distributes itself over the entire skin surface and kills at least 98 percent of the fleas on the animal within 24 hours and will continue to kill fleas for a month. It can withstand water, but not repeated swimming or bathing.

✔ fipronil (such as Frontline) comes as either a spray that you must apply all over the dog's body, or as a self-distributing liquid applied only on the dog's back. Once applied, fipronil collects in the hair follicles and then wicks out over time; thus, it is resistant to being washed off and can kill fleas for up to three months on dogs. It is also effective on ticks for a shorter period.

✔ lufenuron (such as Program) is given as a pill once a month. Fleas that bite the dog and ingest the lufenuron in the dog's system are rendered sterile. It is extremely safe but all animals in the environment must be treated in order for the regime to be effective.

✔ pyriproxyfen (such as Nylar, Sumilar, and others) is an insect growth regulator available as an animal or premise spray. It is marketed in different strengths and formulations, and it can protect in the home or yard for six to twelve months, and on the

1. *sinus cavity*
2. *eye*
3. *brain*
4. *esophagus*
5. *thyroid cartilage*
6. *trachea*
7. *spinal cord*
8. *thymus*
9. *lungs*
10. *heart*
11. *liver*
12. *stomach*
13. *spleen*
14. *kidney*
15. *jejunum*
16. *urether*
17. *colon*
18. *rectum*
19. *bladder*

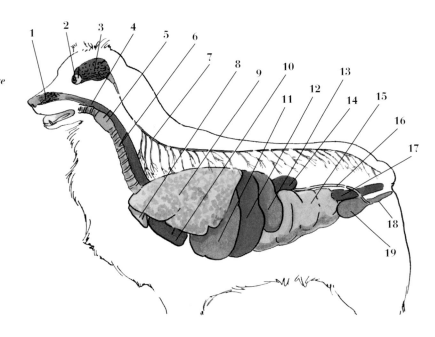

Internal anatomy:

animal for 100 days, depending on the particular product.

Traditional flea control products are either less effective or less safe than these newer products. The permethrins and pyrethrins are safe, but have virtually no residual action. The large family of cholinesterase inhibitors (Dursban, Diazinon, malathion, Sevin, Carbaryl, Pro-Spot, Spotton) last a little longer, but have been known to kill dogs when overused, used in combination with cholinesterase-inhibiting yard products, or with cholinesterase-inhibiting dewormers. Incidentally, the ultrasonic flea-repelling collars have been shown to be both ineffective on fleas and irritating to dogs. Scientific studies have also shown that feeding dogs brewer's yeast or garlic, as has been advocated for years by many dog owners, is ineffective against fleas.

Mites

Two different species of mites cause different forms of mange in dogs. *Sarcoptic mange* causes intense itching, often characterized by scaling of the ear tips. It is highly contagious but can be cured with an insecticidal dip.

Demodectic mange is not contagious, but is far more difficult to cure. The condition tends to run in families, and is more common in certain breeds. It is characterized by a moth-eaten appearance, most often around the eyes and lips. Demodectic mange affecting the feet is also common, and can be extremely resistant to treatment. Most cases of demodectic mange appear in puppies, and most consist of only a few patches that often go away by themselves. In those cases that continue to spread, or in adult-onset demodectic mange, aggressive treatment using an amitraz insecticidal dip is needed. Your veterinarian will need to perform a skin-scraping to confirm the diagnosis before prescribing treatment.

Skin Problems

Flea allergy dermatitis (FAD) is the most common of all skin problems. Itchy, crusted bumps with hair loss in the region around the rump, especially at the base of the tail, results from a flea bite (actually, the flea's saliva) anywhere on the dog's body.

Besides FAD, dogs can have allergic reactions to pollens or other inhaled allergens. Allergies

to weeds can manifest themselves between the dog's toes. Suspect them when you see the dog constantly licking its feet, or when the feet are stained pink from saliva. Food allergies can also occur. New blood tests for antibodies are much easier and less expensive (though not as comprehensive) than the traditional intradermal skin testing.

Pyoderma, with pus-filled bumps and crusting, is another common skin disease. *Impetigo* is characterized by such bumps and crusting most often in the groin area of puppies. Both are treated with antibiotics and antibacterial shampoos.

A reddened, moist, itchy spot that suddenly appears is most likely a *"hot spot" (pyotraumatic dermatitis),* which arises from an itch-scratch-chew cycle resulting most commonly from fleas or flea allergy. Wash the area with an oatmeal-based shampoo, and prevent the dog from further chewing. Use an Elizabethan collar (available from your veterinarian or you can fashion one from a plastic pail), or an antichew preparation such as Bitter Apple (available from most pet stores). Your veterinarian can also prescribe anti-inflammatory medication. As a temporary measure, you can give an allergy pill (Benadryl—ask your veterinarian about dosage), which alleviates some itching and causes drowsiness, both of which should decrease chewing.

In *seborrhea,* there may be excessive dandruff or greasiness, often with excessive earwax and rancid odor. Treatment is with antiseborrheic shampoos or diet change.

Hair may be lost in a bilaterally symmetric

Many skin problems require special shampoos.

Different environments may predispose your dog to special health concerns.

pattern, without itching, due to hypothyroidism, Cushing's syndrome, or testicular tumors.

Doggy odor is not only offensive, it is unnatural. Don't exile the dog, or hold your breath. If a bath doesn't produce results, it's time to use your nose to sniff out the source of the problem. Infection is a common cause of bad odor; check the mouth, ears, feet, and genitals. Generalized bad odor can indicate a skin problem, such as seborrhea. Don't ignore bad odor, and don't make your dog take the blame for something you need to fix.

Internal Parasites

Internal parasites can rob your dog of vital nutrients, good health, and sometimes even a long life. The most common internal parasites set up housekeeping in the intestines and heart.

Nematode Parasites

Hookworms, whipworms, ascarids, threadworms, and lungworms are all types of nematode parasites that can infect dogs of all ages, but have their most devastating effect on puppies. When you take your dog to be vaccinated, bring along a stool specimen so that your veterinarian can also check for these parasites. Most puppies do have worms at some point, even pups from the most fastidious breeders. This is because some types of larval worms become encysted in the dam's body long before she ever became pregnant, perhaps when she herself was a pup. Here they lie dormant and immune from worming, until hormonal changes due to her pregnancy cause them to be activated, and then they infect her fetuses or her newborns through her milk. You may be tempted to pick up some worm medication and worm your puppy yourself, but don't. Over-the-counter wormers are largely ineffective and often more dangerous than those available through your veterinarian. Left untreated, worms can cause vomiting, diarrhea, dull coat, listlessness, anemia, and death. Have your puppy tested for internal parasites regularly. Some heartworm preventives also prevent most types of intestinal worms (but not tapeworms).

Tapeworms (cestodes) tend to plague some dogs throughout their lives. There is no preventive, except to diligently rid your Aussie of fleas, because fleas transmit tapeworms to dogs. Tapeworms look like moving white flat worms on fresh stools, or may dry up and look like rice grains around the dog's anus. They are one of the least debilitating worms, but their segments can be irritating to the dog's anal region, and are certainly unsightly.

Dog owners tend to have some strange ideas concerning worms. Let a dog scoot its rear on the ground, and its owner automatically diagnoses it as "wormy." Although scooting may be a sign of tapeworms, a dog that repeatedly scoots more likely has impacted anal sacs. Somebody somewhere popularized the notion that feeding a dog sugar and sweets will give it worms. There are good reasons not to feed a dog sweets, but worms have nothing to do

with them. And some companies have made a fortune at the expense of dog owners and their dogs by promoting the idea that dogs should be regularly wormed every month or so. Dogs should be wormed when, and only when, they have been diagnosed with worms. No worm medication is completely without risk, and it is foolish to use it carelessly.

Heartworms: Heartworms are a deadly nematode parasite carried by mosquitoes. Wherever mosquitoes are present, dogs should be on heartworm prevention. Several effective types of heartworm preventive are available, with some also preventing many other types of worms. Some require daily administration, while others require only monthly administration. The latter type is more popular and actually has a wider margin of safety and protection. They don't stay in the dog's system for a month, but instead act on a particular stage in the heartworm's development. Giving the drug each month prevents any heartworms from ever maturing. In warm areas your dog may need to be on prevention year-round, but in milder climates your dog may need to use prevention only during the warmer months. Your veterinarian can advise you about when your puppy should start and if year-round prevention is necessary in your area.

Note that Aussies are more sensitive than other breeds to a particular type of monthly preventive, ivermectin. Although it is generally safe for Aussies in the amounts prescribed for heartworm preventive, it has been known to cause toxic reactions in amounts prescribed for heartworm treatment. Many Aussie owners prefer instead to use another monthly preventive, such as milbemycin oxime (sold under the name "Interceptor").

If you forget to give the preventive as prescribed, your dog may get heartworms. A dog with suspected heartworms should not be given the daily preventive because a fatal reaction could occur. The most common way of checking for heartworms is to check the blood for circulating microfilarae (the immature form of heartworms), but this method may fail to detect the presence of adult heartworms in as many as 20 percent of all tested dogs. An "occult" heartworm test, though slightly more expensive, tests for the presence of antigens to heartworms in the blood, and is more accurate. With either test, the presence of heartworms will not be detectable until nearly seven months after infection. Heartworms are treatable in their early stages, but the treatment is expensive and not without risks (although a less risky treatment has recently become available). If untreated, heartworms can kill your pet.

Protozoan Parasites

Puppies and dogs also suffer from protozoan parasites, such as coccidia, and especially *Giardia*. These can cause chronic or intermittent diarrhea, and can be diagnosed with a stool specimen. Because they are not "worms," worm medications are ineffective. Your veterinarian can prescribe appropriate medication.

Vaccinations

Rabies, distemper, leptospirosis, canine hepatitis, parvovirus, and corona virus are highly contagious and deadly diseases that have broken many a loving owner's heart in the past. Now that vaccinations are available for these maladies one would think they would no longer be a threat, but many dogs remain unvaccinated and continue to succumb to and spread these potentially fatal illnesses. Don't let your Aussie be one of them.

Puppies receive their dam's immunity through nursing in the first days of life. This is why it is important that your pup's mother be properly immunized long before breeding, and that your pup be able to nurse from its dam. The immunity gained from the mother will wear off after several weeks, and then the pup will be susceptible to disease unless you provide immunity through vaccinations. The problem is that there is no way to know exactly when this passive immunity will wear off, and vaccinations given before that time are ineffective; therefore, you must revaccinate over a period of weeks so that your pup will not be unprotected and will receive effective immunity.

Your pup's breeder will have given the first vaccinations to your pup before it was old enough to go home with you. Bring all

Sample Vaccination Schedule

Age (weeks)	Vaccine
6 to 8	distemper + hepatitis + parainfluenza + parvovirus
10 to 12	distemper + hepatitis + parainfluenza + parvovirus + leptospirosis
14 to 16	distemper + hepatitis + parainfluenza + parvovirus + leptospirosis, rabies
18 to 20	distemper + hepatitis + parainfluenza + parvovirus + leptospirosis

Why Breeding Is a Bad Idea

Many more good Aussies are born than there are good homes available. The puppy you sell to a less-than-perfect home may end up neglected, abused, discarded, or returned. Aussies typically have from five to seven puppies. Breeding so you can keep one pup ignores the fact that six others may not get a good home—or may be ransacking your home for the next ten years.

Unless your Aussie has proven itself by earning titles and awards in competitions, or by being an outstanding working stockdog, you will have a difficult time finding buyers. Selling puppies will not come close to reimbursing you for the stud fee, prenatal care, whelping complications, cesarean sections, supplemental feeding, puppy food, vaccinations, advertising, and a staggering amount of time and energy.

Responsible breeders spend years researching genetics and the breed, breed only the best specimens, and screen for hereditary defects in order to obtain superior puppies. Unless you have done the same, you are doing yourself, your dog, the puppies, any buyers, and the breed a great disservice.

If you must breed your Aussie, please invest in a book about the mechanics of breeding. Too many uninformed breeders allow their dogs to suffer and even die because they don't have proper information.

information about your pup's vaccination history to your veterinarian on your first visit so that the pup's vaccination schedule can be maintained. Meanwhile, it is best not to let your pup mingle with strange dogs.

Recent studies have implicated repeated vaccinations with combinations of vaccines with some immune system problems. Some veterinarians thus recommend staggering different types of vaccines, and discourage overvaccination. They also discourage vaccination in any dog that is under stress or not well. Many dogs seem to feel under the weather for a day or so after getting their vaccinations, so don't schedule your appointment the day before boarding, a trip, or a big doggy event.

Vaccinations are also available for kennel cough and Lyme disease, but may be optional depending upon your dog's lifestyle. In fact, in most parts of the country, the possibility of complications due to the Lyme vaccine are greater than the probability of problems due to actually contracting Lyme disease. Your veterinarian can advise you.

Neutering and Spaying

If you don't intend to breed your pet—and there are more good reasons not to breed than to breed—plan to schedule this simple surgery before your pet reaches puberty, at least by eight or nine months of age. Not only will you not be contributing to the pet overpopulation problem, but you will be helping to safeguard your Aussie's life.

1. Spaying (surgical removal of ovaries and uterus) before the first season drastically reduces the chances of breast or uterine cancer.

Their well-being is in your hands. Don't let them down.

2. Castration (surgical removal of the testicles) virtually eliminates the chance of testicular or prostate cancer.

3. Dogs with undescended testicles have an increased risk of testicular cancer, and should be castrated before three to five years of age.

4. In a recent study, 80 percent of all dogs killed by automobiles were intact (unneutered) males, apparently making their rounds.

HOW–TO: GROOMING

Brushing

Most Aussies have medium-length hair that should be brushed at least once a week. A slicker brush removes dead hair; in periods of intense shedding you can also use a shedding blade. Use a pin brush if you are trying to save coat. Be sure to brush down to the skin, and don't neglect the areas behind the ears or under the armpits—both prime sites for mats. If you find a mat, spray it with a detangler and try to split it lengthwise and then split it again. Remember to brush the hair out of the mat, not the mat out of the hair.

Bathing

Dog skin has a pH of 7.5, while human skin has a pH of 5.5; therefore, bathing in a shampoo formulated for the pH of human skin can lead to scaling and irritation. You will generally get better results with a shampoo made for dogs. Most shampoos will kill fleas even if not especially formulated as a flea shampoo, but none has any residual killing action on fleas, so, in general, flea shampoos are not a good buy. No dog owner should be without one of the shampoos that requires no water or rinsing; these are wonderful for puppies, spot-baths, and emergencies.

Several therapeutic shampoos are available for various skin problems. Dry scaly skin: moisturizing shampoos; excessive scale and dandruff: antiseborrheic shampoos; damaged skin: antimicrobials; itchy skin: oatmeal-based antipruritics.

Ear Care

The dog's ear canal is made up of an initial long vertical segment that then abruptly angles to run horizontally toward the skull. This configuration provides a moist environment in which various ear infections can flourish, especially in a dog with hanging ears. It is fairly simple to keep the Aussie's ears healthy by checking them regularly and not allowing moisture or debris to build up in them.

Signs of ear problems include inflammation, discharge, debris, foul odor, pain, scratching, shaking, tilting of the head, or circling to one side. Extreme pain may indicate a ruptured eardrum. Ear problems can be difficult to cure once they have become established, so early veterinary attention is crucial. Bacterial and fungal infections, ear mites or ticks, foreign bodies, inhalant allergies, seborrhea, or hypothyroidism are possible underlying problems. Grass

awns are one of the most common causes of ear problems in dogs that spend time outdoors. Keep the ear lubricated with mineral oil, and seek veterinary treatment as soon as possible.

Ear mites, which are often found in puppies, are highly contagious and intensely irritating. Affected dogs will shake their head, scratch their ears, and carry their head sideways. The ear mite's signature is a dark, dry, waxy buildup resembling coffee grounds in the ear canal, usually of both ears. This material is actually dried blood mixed with earwax. Over-the-counter ear mite preparations can cause worse irritation; therefore, ear mites are best treated by your veterinarian.

Apply ear mite drops daily for at least a week, and possibly a month. Because these mites are also found in the dog's fur, you should also bathe the pet weekly with a pyrethrin-based shampoo, or apply a pyrethrin flea dip, powder, or spray.

Nail Care

You must trim your dog's nails every week or two to prevent discomfort or even lameness.

Begin by cutting the very tips of your puppy's nails every week, taking special care not to cut the "quick" (the central

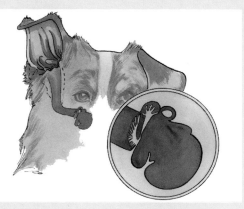

The ear canal.

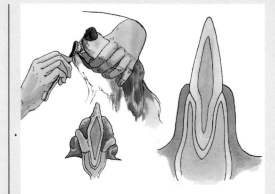

It is important to brush your Aussie's teeth to prevent infection from plaque and tartar. Left: an infected tooth. Right: a healthy tooth.

core of blood vessels and nerve endings). You may find it easiest to cut the nails by holding the foot backwards, much as a horse's hoof is held when being shod. This way your Aussie can't see what's going on, and you can see the bottom of the nail. Here you will see a solid core culminating in a hollowed nail. Cut the tip up to the core, but not beyond. On occasion you will slip up and cause the nail to bleed, which is best stopped by styptic powder; if this is not available, dip the nail in flour or hold a wet tea bag to it.

Dental Care

Tooth plaque and tartar contribute to bad breath and health problems. Dry food and hard dog biscuits, rawhide and nylabone chewies are helpful, but not totally effective, at removing plaque. Brushing your Aussie's teeth once or twice weekly (optimally daily) with a child's toothbrush and *doggy toothpaste* is the best plaque remover. If not removed, plaque will attract bacteria and minerals, which will harden into tartar. If you cannot brush, your veterinarian can supply a cleansing solution that will

help to kill plaque-forming bacteria. You may have to have your veterinarian clean your dog's teeth as often as once a year.

Neglected plaque and tartar can cause infections to form along the gum line. The infection can gradually work its way down the sides of the tooth until the entire root is undermined. The tissues and bone around the tooth erode, and the tooth finally falls out. Meanwhile, the bacteria may have entered the bloodstream and traveled throughout the body, causing infection in the kidneys and heart valves. Neglecting your dog's teeth could kill your dog.

Between four and seven months of age, Aussie puppies will begin to shed their baby teeth. Often, deciduous (baby) teeth, especially the canines (fangs), are not shed, so that the permanent tooth grows in beside the baby tooth. If this condition persists for over a week, consult your veterinarian. Retained baby teeth can cause misalignment of adult teeth. Correct occlusion is important for good dental health. In a correct Aussie bite, the top incisors should fit snugly in front of the bottom incisors.

Your home care maintenance can go only so far in ensuring your Aussie's healthy status. No matter how diligent you are, eventually your Aussie will need professional medical attention. A good veterinarian will also be needed to monitor your dog's internal signs by way of blood tests and other procedures.

Choosing a Veterinarian

When choosing your veterinarian, consider availability, emergency arrangements, costs, facilities, and ability to communicate. Some veterinarians will include more sophisticated tests as part of their regular checkups. Such tests, while desirable, will add to the cost of a visit. Unless money is no object, reach an understanding about procedures and fees before having them performed. You and your veterinarian will form a team that will work together to protect your Aussie's health, so your rapport with your veterinarian is very important. Your veterinarian should listen to your observations, and should explain to you exactly what is happening with your dog. The clinic should be clean, and have safe, sanitary overnight accommodations. After-hours emergency arrangements should be made clear. A veterinarian who is familiar with Aussies is a real asset, but not essential.

Make sure your Aussie is as healthy on the inside as it appears on the outside.

Blood Work

Your Aussie's blood can provide valuable clues about its state of health, which is why your veterinarian will often want a blood sample if your dog is ill. In fact, it is a good idea to have blood values for your Aussie when it is well as a source of later comparison if it ever becomes ill. Also, you should insist on such blood tests before your pet undergoes surgery to ensure that it is healthy enough for the procedure. The most common tests are the complete blood count (CBC) and the blood chemistry test ("Chem panel"). Many other specialized tests are fairly common.

Emergency Situations

Even experienced dog owners have a difficult time deciding what constitutes a true emergency; when in doubt, err on the side of caution and call the emergency clinic or your veterinarian for an opinion.

Be Prepared

Because there are no paramedics for dogs, you must assume the role of paramedic and ambulance driver in case of an emergency. Now is the time to prepare for these life-saving roles. Know the phone number and location of the emergency veterinarian in your area. Keep the number next to the phone; don't rely on your memory during an emergency situation. Study the emergency procedures described in

Common Blood Tests

CBC Reports

Component	Significance
Red blood cells	cells responsible for carrying oxygen throughout the body
White blood cells	infection-fighting cells
Platelets	components responsible for clotting blood to stop bleeding

Blood Chemistry Test Reports

Component	Significance
Albumin (ALB)	reduced levels are suggestive of liver or kidney disease, or parasites
Alanine aminotransferase (ALT)	elevated levels suggest liver disease
Alkaline phosphatase (ALKP)	elevated levels can indicate liver disease or Cushing's syndrome
Amylase (AMYL)	elevated levels suggest pancreatic or kidney disease
Blood urea nitrogen (BUN)	elevated levels suggest kidney disease
Calcium (CA)	elevated levels suggest kidney or parathyroid disease or some types of tumors
Cholesterol (CHOL)	elevated levels suggest liver or kidney disease or several other disorders
Creatinine (CREA)	elevated levels suggest kidney disease or urinary obstruction
Blood Glucose (GLU)	low levels can suggest liver disease
Phosphorous (PHOS)	elevated levels can suggest kidney disease
Total bilirubin (TBIL)	level can indicate problems in the bile ducts
Total protein (TP)	level can indicate problems of the liver, kidney, or gastrointestinal tract.

this chapter, and keep this guide handy. Misplaced instructions can result in the loss of critical time. Always keep enough fuel in your car to make it to the emergency clinic without stopping for gas. Finally, stay calm. It will help you help your dog, and will help your dog stay calm as well. A calm dog is less likely to go into shock.

For the following situations, administer first aid and seek veterinary attention.

Poisoning

Symptoms and treatment vary depending upon the specific poison. In most cases, home treatment is not advisable. If in doubt about whether poison was ingested, call the veterinarian anyway. If possible, bring the poison and its container with you to the veterinarian.

Two of the most common and life-threatening poisons eaten by dogs are Warfarin (rodent poison) and, especially, ethylene glycol (antifreeze).

Veterinary treatment must be obtained within two to four hours of ingestion of even tiny amounts of these substances if the dog's life is to be saved. *Do not wait for symptoms.* By the time symptoms of antifreeze poisoning are evident, it is usually too late to save the dog.

Signs of poisoning vary according to the type of poison, but commonly include vomiting, convulsions, staggering, and collapse.

Call the veterinary poison control hotline (1-900-680-0000 or 1-800-548-2423; note that calls will incur a $20 to $30 charge) and give as much information as possible. Induce vomiting (except in the cases outlined below) by giving either hydrogen peroxide (mixed 1:1 with water), saltwater, or dry mustard and water. Treat for shock and get the dog to the veterinarian at once. Be prepared for convulsions or respiratory distress.

Do not induce vomiting if the poison was an acid, alkali, petroleum product, solvent, cleaner, tranquilizer, or if a sharp object was swallowed; also do not induce vomiting if the dog is severely depressed, convulsing, comatose, or if over two hours have passed since ingestion. If the dog is not convulsing or unconscious: dilute the poison by giving milk, vegetable oil, or egg whites. Activated charcoal can adsorb many toxins. Baking soda or milk of magnesia can be given for ingested acids, and vinegar or lemon juice for ingested alkalis.

Seizures

A dog undergoing a seizure may drool, become stiff, or have uncontrollable muscle spasms.

Wrap the dog securely in a blanket to prevent it from injuring itself on furniture or stairs. Remove other dogs from the area (they

Steps to Take in an Emergency

✔ Make sure you and the dog are in a safe location.
✔ Make sure breathing passages are open. Remove any collar and check the mouth and throat.
✔ Move the dog as little and as gently as possible.
✔ Control any bleeding.
✔ Check breathing, pulse, and consciousness.
✔ Check for signs of shock (very pale gums, weakness, unresponsiveness, faint pulse, shivering). Treat by keeping the dog warm and calm.
✔ Never use force or do anything that causes extreme discomfort.
✔ Never remove an impaled object (unless it is blocking the airway).

may attack the convulsing dog). Never put your hands—or anything—in a convulsing dog's mouth. Treat for shock. Make note of all characteristics and sequences of seizure activity, which can help to diagnose the cause.

Snakebites

Poisonous snakebites are characterized by swelling, discoloration, pain, fangmarks, restlessness, nausea, and weakness.

Restrain the dog and keep it quiet. Be able to describe the snake. Only if you can't get to the veterinarian immediately, apply a pressure bandage (not a tourniquet but a firm bandage) between the bite and the heart. If on a leg, keep it lower than the rest of the body. Most bites are on the head, and are difficult to treat with first aid.

Your Aussie should be comfortable at the veterinarian's office.

Allergic Reaction

Insect stings are the most common cause of extreme reactions. Swelling around the nose and throat can block the airway. Other possible reactions include restlessness, vomiting, diarrhea, seizures, and collapse. If any of these symptoms occur, immediate veterinary attention will probably be necessary.

Bleeding

Consider wounds to be an emergency if there is profuse bleeding, if they are extremely deep, or if they open to the chest cavity, abdominal cavity, or head.

Control massive bleeding first. Cover the wound with a clean dressing and apply pressure; apply more dressings over the others until the bleeding stops. Also elevate the wound site, and apply a cold pack to the site. If an extremity is involved, apply pressure to the closest pressure point as follows:

✔ For a front leg: inside of the front leg just above the elbow.

✔ For a rear leg: inside of the thigh where the femoral artery crosses the thighbone.

Use a tourniquet only in life-threatening situations and when all other attempts have failed. Check for signs of shock.

Sucking chest wounds: Place a sheet of plastic or other nonporous material over the hole and bandage it to make as airtight a seal as possible.

Abdominal wounds: Place a warm, wet, sterile dressing over any protruding internal organs; cover with a bandage or towel. Do not attempt to push organs back into the dog.

Head wounds: Apply gentle pressure to control bleeding. Monitor for loss of consciousness or shock and treat accordingly.

Burns

Deep burns, characterized by charred or pearly white skin, with deeper layers of tissue exposed, are serious.

Cool the burned area with cool packs, towels soaked in water, or by immersing in cold water. If over 50 percent of the dog is burned, however, do not immerse as this increases the likelihood of shock. Cover with a clean bandage or towel to avoid contamination. Do not apply pressure; do not apply ointments. Monitor for shock.

Holidays are prime times for poisoning, overeating, and accidents.

Electrical Shock

A dog that chews an electric cord may collapse and have burns inside its mouth.

Before touching the dog, disconnect the plug or cut the electrical power; if that cannot be done immediately, use a *wooden* pencil, spoon, or broom handle to knock the cord away from the dog. Keep the dog warm and treat for shock. Monitor breathing and heartbeat.

Heatstroke

Rapid, loud breathing, abundant thick saliva, bright red mucous membranes, and a high rectal temperature are earlier signs of heatstroke. Later signs include unsteadiness, diarrhea, and coma.

Wet the dog down and place it in front of a fan. If this is not possible, immerse the dog in cool water. *Do not plunge the dog in ice water;* the resulting constriction of peripheral blood vessels can make the situation worse. Offer small amounts of water for drinking. You must lower your dog's body temperature quickly, but do not lower it below 100°F (37.8°C). Stop cooling the dog when its temperature reaches 103°F (39.4°C).

Hypothermia

Shivering, cold-feeling, and sluggishness are signs of a dog that has become excessively chilled. Later signs include a very low—under 95°F (35°C)—body temperature, slow pulse and breathing rates, and coma.

Warm the dog gradually. Wrap it in a blanket (preferably one that has been warmed in the dryer). Place plastic bottles filled with hot water outside the blankets (not touching the dog). You can also place a plastic tarp over the blanket, making sure the dog's head is not covered. Monitor the temperature. Stop warming when the temperature reaches 101°F (38.3°C).

Hypoglycemia (Low Blood Sugar)

A dog with low blood sugar may appear disoriented, weak, staggering, and perhaps blind. Its muscles may twitch. Later stages lead to convulsions, coma, and death.

Give food, or honey or syrup mixed with warm water.

Situations not described in this list can usually be treated with the same first aid as for humans. In all cases, it is best to seek the opinion of a veterinarian.

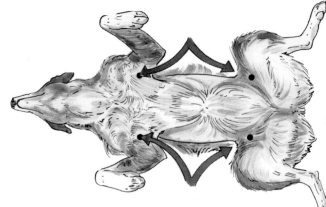

Pressure points.

Consult your veterinarian immediately if your dog vomits a foul substance resembling fecal matter (indicating a blockage in the intestinal tract), blood (partially digested blood resembling coffee grounds), or if there is projectile or continued vomiting. Sporadic vomiting with poor appetite and generally poor condition could indicate internal parasites or a more serious internal disease.

Sickness

If a problem persists for more than a couple of days, it is worth getting your veterinarian's opinion. Following is an outline of the most common symptoms and some of their possible causes.

Vomiting

Vomiting is a common occurrence that may or may not indicate a serious problem. Vomiting after eating grass is not unusual and usually of no great concern. Overeating is a common cause of occasional vomiting in puppies, especially if they follow eating with playing. Feed smaller meals more frequently if this becomes a problem. Vomiting immediately after meals could indicate an obstruction of the esophagus. Repeated vomiting could indicate that the dog has eaten spoiled food, undigestible objects, or may have a gastrointestinal problem. Veterinary advice should be sought. Meanwhile, withhold food (or feed as directed for diarrhea), and restrict water.

Diarrhea

Diarrhea can result from overexcitement or nervousness, a change in diet or water, sensitivity to certain foods, overeating, intestinal parasites, viral or bacterial infections, or ingestion of toxic substances. Bloody diarrhea, diarrhea with vomiting, fever, or other signs of toxicity, or a diarrhea that lasts for more than a day should not be allowed to continue without veterinary advice. Some of these could be symptomatic of potentially fatal disorders.

Less severe diarrhea can be treated at home by withholding or severely restricting food and water for 24 hours. Ice cubes can be given to satisfy thirst. Administer human diarrhea medication in the same weight dosage as recommended for humans. A bland diet consisting of rice, tapioca, or cooked macaroni, along with cottage cheese or tofu for protein, should be given for several days. Feed nothing else. The intestinal tract needs time off in order to heal.

Coughing

Allergies, foreign bodies, pneumonia, parasites, tracheal collapse, tumors, and especially kennel cough and heart disease can all cause coughing.

Kennel cough is a highly communicable air-borne disease caused by several different infectious agents. It is characterized by a gagging cough arising about a week after exposure. Inoculations are available and are an especially good idea if you plan to have your dog around other dogs at training classes or while being boarded.

Heart disease can result in coughing, most often following exercise or in the evening. Affected dogs will often lie down and point their nose in the air in order to breathe better.

Any persistent cough should be checked by your veterinarian.

Urinary Tract Diseases

If your dog has difficulty or pain in urination, urinates suddenly and often but in small amounts, or passes cloudy or bloody urine, it may be suffering from an ailment of the bladder, urethra, or prostate. Dribbling of urine during sleep can indicate a hormonal problem. Urinalysis and a rectal exam by your veterinarian are necessary to diagnose the exact nature of the problem. Bladder infections must be treated promptly to prevent the infection from reaching the kidneys.

Blockage of urine can result in death. Inability to urinate requires immediate emergency veterinary attention.

Kidney disease, ultimately leading to kidney failure, is one of the most common ailments of older dogs. The earliest symptom is usually increased urination. Although the excessive urination may cause problems in keeping your house clean or your night's sleep intact, never try to restrict water from a dog with kidney disease. Increased urination can also be a sign of diabetes or a urinary tract infection. Your veterinarian can discover the cause with some simple tests, and each of these conditions can be treated. For kidney disease, a low-protein and low-sodium diet can slow the progression.

In males, infections of the *prostate gland* can lead to repeated urinary tract infections, and sometimes painful defecation or blood and pus in the urine. Castration and long-term antibiotic therapy is required for improvement.

Impacted Anal Sacs

Constant licking of the anus or scooting of the anus along the ground are characteristic signs of anal sac impaction. Dogs have two anal sacs that are normally emptied by rectal pressure during defecation. Their musky-smelling contents may also be forcibly ejected when a dog is extremely frightened. Sometimes they fail to empty properly and become impacted or infected. This is more common in obese dogs, dogs with allergies or seborrhea, and dogs that seldom have firm stools. Impacted sacs cause extreme discomfort and can become infected. Treatment consists of manually emptying the sacs and administering antibiotics. As a last resort, the sacs may be removed surgically.

Endocrine Disorders

The most widespread hormone-related disorders in the dog are diabetes, hypothyroidism, and Cushing's syndrome. The most common of these, *hypothyroidism,* also has the least obvious symptoms, which may include weight gain, lethargy, and coat problems such as oiliness, dullness, *symmetrical* hair loss, and hair that is easily pulled out.

The hallmark of *diabetes* is increased drinking and urination, and sometimes increased appetite with weight loss.

Cushing's syndrome (hyperadrenocorticism) is seen mostly in older dogs, and is characterized by increased drinking and urination, pot-bellied appearance, symmetrical hair loss on the body, darkened skin, and susceptibility to infections.

All of these conditions can be diagnosed with simple tests, and can be treated with drugs by your veterinarian.

Bites and Stings

If your dog is bitten, allow some bleeding, then clean the area thoroughly and apply antibiotic ointment. A course of oral antibiotics will probably be necessary. It's best not to

Be prepared to administer home health care but don't hesitate to seek veterinary advice.

suture most animal bites, but a large one—over ¹/₂ inch (13 mm) in diameter—or one on the face or other prominent position may need to be sutured.

Dogs are often stung by insects on their face or feet. Remove any visible stingers as quickly as possible. Administer baking soda and water paste to bee stings, and vinegar to wasp stings. Clean the area and apply antibacterial ointment. Keep an eye on the dog in case it has an allergic reaction; if it does, immediately call your veterinarian.

Eye Problems

Aussies generally have healthy eyes, but are subject to several hereditary eye disorders (see page 14). An exam by a veterinary ophthalmologist is essential for any Aussie contemplated as breeding stock.

Squinting or tearing can be due to an irritated cornea or foreign body. Examine under the lids and flood the eye with saline solution, or use a moist cotton swab to remove any debris. If no improvement is seen after a day, have your veterinarian take a look. A watery discharge without squinting can be a symptom of allergies or a tear drainage problem. A clogged tear drainage duct can cause the tears to drain onto the face rather than the normal drainage through the nose. Your veterinarian can diagnose a drainage problem with a simple test.

For contact with eye irritants, flush the eye for five minutes with water or saline solution. For injuries, cover with clean gauze soaked in water or saline solution.

As your Aussie ages, it is natural that the lens of the eye becomes a little hazy; you will notice this as a slightly grayish appearance behind the pupils. If this occurs at a young age, or if the lens looks white or opaque, ask your veterinarian to check your dog for *cataracts*. In cataracts the lens becomes so opaque that light can no longer reach the retina; as in humans, the lens can be surgically replaced with an artificial lens.

Any time your dog's pupils do not react to light or when one eye reacts differently from another, take it to the veterinarian immediately. It could indicate a serious ocular or neurological problem. The eyes are such complex and sensitive organs; you should always be cautious and seek veterinary help.

The Medicine Chest

✔ rectal thermometer
✔ scissors
✔ tweezers
✔ sterile gauze dressings
✔ self-adhesive bandage (such as Vet-Wrap)
✔ instant cold compress
✔ antidiarrhea medication
✔ ophthalmic ointment
✔ soap
✔ antiseptic skin ointment
✔ hydrogen peroxide
✔ clean sponge
✔ pen light
✔ syringe
✔ towel
✔ stethoscope (optional)
✔ oxygen (optional)
✔ first aid instructions
✔ veterinarian and emergency clinic numbers
✔ poison control center number

Giving Medication

When giving pills, open your dog's mouth and place the pill well to the back and in the middle of the tongue. Close the mouth and gently stroke the throat until your dog swallows. Pre-wetting capsules or covering them with cream cheese or some other food helps prevent capsules from sticking to the tongue or roof of the mouth. For liquid medicine, tilt the head back, keep the dog's mouth almost (but not quite tightly) closed and place the liquid in the pouch of the cheek. Then hold the mouth closed until the dog swallows. Always give the full course of medications prescribed by your veterinarian. Don't give your dog human medications unless you have been directed to do so by your veterinarian.

HOW-TO: FIRST AID

In an emergency, first check to see if the dog is responsive by calling its name or tapping on its head. If it is not, quickly assess the ABCs of first aid:

A: Airway
B: Breathing
C: Circulation

Airway: Make sure the airway is open. Extend the head and neck, open the mouth, and pull the tongue forward.

Breathing: Make sure the dog is breathing. Is the chest rising and falling? Can you feel exhaled air against your cheek? If not, give two rapid breaths through the dog's nose before checking circulation.

Circulation: Check gum color, capillary refill time, and pulse. Gum color should be pink. When you press your thumb on the gum, it should regain its color within two sec-onds. Check the pulse by feeling either the heartbeat on the left side of the rib cage a couple of inches behind the elbow or the pulse on the inside of the thigh, near the groin.

If your dog has a pulse, but is not breathing, administer artificial respiration.

If your dog does not have a pulse, administer cardiopulmonary resuscitation (CPR)

Artificial Respiration

1. Open the dog's mouth; clear passage of secretions and foreign bodies.

2. Pull the dog's tongue forward.

3. Seal your mouth over the dog's nose and mouth, blow into the dog's nose for two seconds, then release.

4. You should see your dog's chest expand; if not, try blowing with more force, making a tighter seal around the lips, or checking for an obstruction (see following).

5. Repeat at a rate of one breath every four seconds.

6. Stop every minute to monitor breathing and pulse.

7. If air collects in the stomach, push down just behind the rib cage every few minutes.

8. Continue until the dog breathes on its own.

Checking the airway.

Check the pulse at the femoral artery.

Normal Values

Respiration:	10–30 breaths per minute at rest
Pulse:	60–120 beats per minute at rest
Temperature:	101.5–102.5°F (38–39°C)
Capillary refill time:	Less than 2 seconds
Gum color:	Pink (not white, red, bluish, yellowish, or with tiny red spots)
Hydration:	Skin should pop back into position within 3 seconds of being lifted

For obstructions, wrap your hands around the abdomen, behind the rib cage, and compress briskly. Repeat if needed. If the dog loses consciousness, extend the head and neck forward, pull the tongue out fully, and explore the throat for any foreign objects.

If due to drowning, turn dog upside down, holding around its waist, and sway back and forth so that water can run out of its mouth. Then administer mouth-to-nose respiration, with the dog's head positioned lower than its lungs.

For any type of emergency, administer the necessary first aid treatment and seek veterinary help *immediately*. If possible, call the veterinary clinic first so they can be prepared for your arrival. In general, always remember the following:

✔ Be calm and reassuring; a calm dog is less likely to go into shock.
✔ Move the dog as little and as gently as possible.
✔ If the dog is in pain, it may bite. Apply a makeshift muzzle with a bandage or tape. Do not muzzle if the dog is having breathing difficulties.

CPR

1. Place your hands, one on top of the other, on the left side of the chest about 2 inches (5 cm) up from and behind the point of the elbow.
2. Press down quickly and release.
3. Compress at a rate of about 100 times per minute.
4. After every 15 compressions give two breaths through the nose. If you have a partner, the partner can give breaths every two or three compressions.

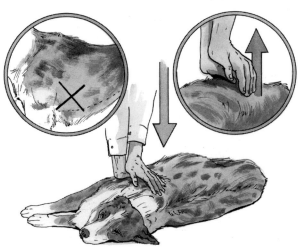

CPR positioning.

TRAINING FOR STOCK WORK

Aussies like to play and love to love, but everything pales compared to the chance to work stock. The sight of a group of animals awakens their driving drive, and it's as though they are transformed back to the western plains. Many working ranches rely on their Australian Shepherds day in and day out to gather, drive, and control their sheep or cattle. Other Aussie owners enjoy competing with their dogs at organized herding trials. Many people think of Border Collies when they think of herding dogs, but the Aussie is a somewhat tougher character, more adept at working cattle or uncooperative sheep. Its technique differs from the Border Collie, tending to work closer to the stock and with a higher head carriage.

Despite its strong instincts, even the best Aussie needs guidance and training. The best way for an inexperienced Aussie owner to train a new dog is to work with an experienced herding dog trainer. You will be able to benefit not only from their years of experience, but also their dog-broke stock (see page 78) and herding facilities. With the growing popularity of herding as a pastime rather than strictly as a utilitarian necessity, finding a herding club or class is becoming increasingly easy. The ASCA

Despite modern technology, the dog remains the shepherd's best helper.

can give you local contacts that can in turn direct you to reputable trainers. If you cannot find anyone to help you, you may have to tackle it on your own.

Preliminary Training

Some trainers suggest letting your young pup grow accustomed to interacting with ducks at a young age. The youngster can practice some rudimentary herding skills, but you must take care that the ducks do not turn the tables on your impressionable puppy! If the pup becomes too rough with the ducks, simply remove it from them without harsh corrections, which could dampen its enthusiasm. Many trainers advocate postponing any work with stock until the dog is 10 to 12 months old. There is plenty of preliminary work to keep both of you busy meanwhile. Some commands are best taught with no stock around. Your dog should know (at least) how to *down, stay,* and *come,* and should also know *"That Will Do"* (or *"OK"*). These commands can be taught just as they are for standard obedience (see pages 39–43). You may also be able to practice the *steady* command away from stock. The other commands are easier to teach while actually working with stock (although some innovative trainers teach these commands using a toy or ball on the end of a fishing pole-type arrangement). You should practice these commands around all types of distractions except stock; when your dog is finally introduced to stock it will probably be somewhat out of control and may ignore your commands. This is to be expected and is no cause for you to despair.

Equipment

Once you feel it is time to introduce your Aussie to real stock, you will need:

1. Stock, preferably ducks or sheep.

2. Working pen. For sheep, this is ideally a round or oval pen about 50 to 70 feet (15 to 21 m) in diameter and clear of trees and bushes. Pens for ducks can be smaller.

Commands

✔ *"Down"*: used to stop the dog. It may later be modified to *"Sit"* or *"Stop."*

✔ *"Stay"*: used to tell the dog to remain in position where it is.

✔ *"Come"*: used to tell the dog to come toward you.

✔ *"Walk Up"*: used to move the dog directly toward the stock.

✔ *"Come Bye"*: used to move the dog in a clockwise direction around the stock.

✔ *"Away to Me"*: used to move the dog in a counterclockwise direction around the stock.

✔ *"Steady"*: used to slow the dog.

✔ *"Get Out"*: used to tell the dog to move away from the stock.

✔ *"Look Back"*: used to tell the dog to look behind it, usually to alert it to a straggling animal.

✔ *"That Will Do"*: used to release the dog from work and call it off the stock.

3. Crook. You can make one out of ½-inch PVC pipe cut to a length of about 5 feet (1.5 m).

4. Long line. You can also make this out of thin (about ¼ inch) rope with a bolt snap at one end and a knot at the other, with a total length of about 15 to 20 feet (4.6 to 6.1 m).

Stock

You will want to start with at least five to ten head of stock. Larger stock should be "dog-broke," meaning it is already experienced with being worked by dogs. Dog-broke stock may be available from herding dog trainers or other enthusiasts, or local enthusiasts may be willing to have their experienced herding dogs practice on your wild bunch. Even so, don't get the first sheep you find. Sheep breeds, like dog breeds, tend to differ in temperament; Dorset crosses are among the easiest to work. Some dogs that are fearful of larger stock may do better with ducks, and ducks are easier to keep. Indian Runners are a good breed of duck for herding. Cattle are best left for later in training, and even then it is best to begin training with calves or goats. Special precautions must be taken with cattle because they can seriously injure your dog—or worse. These precautions include making sure your dog is not working between the cattle and a fence that could trap your dog, and removing your dog's collar so it cannot become entangled in a hoof. Cattle are easier to control if they are already moving when your dog approaches them. Remember that if you get your own stock you will need to care for them and provide food, shelter, and veterinary care.

Although we will use sheep in our training examples, keep in mind that you can also use other species, as well as other techniques.

Basic Stock Work

By sprinkling some grain on the ground you can encourage the sheep to stay together in the center of the pen. An assistant is handy for the first few sessions for releasing the dog. Your dog should also drag the long line (attached to a buckle collar) behind for these first sessions.

Introduction to Stock

You have several major goals to reach with your first few sessions. First of all, you want your Aussie to enjoy the experience. You don't want your dog to be scared of the stock, you, or your crook. Most dogs have a tendency to get in too close to the sheep. If this happens, push the dog away, with the crook if necessary, and yell *"Get out!"* Try to use the least force necessary to get the dog away from the sheep. If the dog continues to go at the sheep, position yourself between the sheep and the dog and, as the dog circles, walk in a smaller circle so that you are always between them, pushing the dog out with the crook as necessary. Many pups will race crazily around the sheep, perhaps jumping in and nipping at them. As long as the dog is not hurting the sheep it's usually best to just let it get this initial excitement out of its system. If the dog is really too rough it may be best to postpone training until it is a little older, or accustom the dog to wearing a muzzle and have it wear it while training. If you use too much force you may

Training the beginning herder to "get out!"

sour the dog on the whole activity. It is easier to get rambunctious dogs off stock than to encourage timid dogs to approach stock.

The Balance Point

Your second general goal is to help your Aussie learn to find the balance point, which is the point at which the sheep attend to the dog without running from it. Remember that although the instinct to herd sheep is strong in your Aussie, the knowledge of how to herd is not. At first your Aussie will experiment a bit, just as you would if trying to manage a group of sheep. You would find that if you ran head-long into them they would disperse and get out of control. You would find that if you stayed too far away from them they would ignore you and be just as out of your control. At some point you would come to realize that the best way is to approach slowly until you find the balance point; that is, the point at which the sheep are watching you and responding to you without moving away. By moving closer to the sheep from that balance point, they would move away from you, but in a controlled manner. This is what your Aussie must learn, and part of that learning is going to come from trial and error,

but it should come to realize that the directions you are giving it are helping it to achieve that balance point and control the sheep.

Keeping a flock of ducks under control is harder than it looks.

Driving Versus Gathering

The first specific goal is to eventually have your dog circle the stock. How you achieve this depends on whether your dog naturally tends to drive or gather. Gathering dogs will instinctively tend to position themselves on the opposite side of the flock from you. This means that if you move in a clockwise direction, your dog will do the same in order to keep directly opposite you. By always saying "*Come Bye*" before moving in a clockwise direction, and "*Away to Me*" before moving in a counterclockwise direction, your dog will soon learn the meaning of those commands.

Driving dogs tend to push stock away from the handler and will position themselves between the handler and the sheep. You must block the dog from coming straight into the sheep, either with your arms or the crook as an extension of your arms. The dog will circle out around the sheep in order to avoid you. Be sure

to stay between the dog and the sheep, following along slightly behind it in a circle around the sheep. To have the dog turn and circle in the opposite direction, get in front of the dog and walk toward it, giving the appropriate flanking command ("*Come Bye*" or "*Away to Me*"). Use the crook to guide the dog, not hit it. Whichever method you use, it is best if you keep the dog moving at this point. If it stops, then the sheep stop, and this encourages new dogs to run into their midst and scatter them.

Each session should last only about ten minutes. At the end of the session, take the dog by the long line, say "*That will do*," and lead it away from the sheep (not through them). Practice this initial lesson until your dog is circling the sheep and responding to your flanking commands. After a few sessions your dog should be ready for more advanced lessons.

Advanced Stock Work

Fetch: To teach the fetch, position yourself with the sheep between you and the dog and have the dog *down*. Then back away from the sheep so that they move toward you. Call the dog and say "*Walk up.*" The dog should ease toward the sheep. If the dog doesn't move, you can pull it with the long line. If it rushes the sheep, you will have to push it off. If the dog tries to circle the sheep, meet it head on so that it stops and changes direction. It may be easiest to practice with the sheep along one side of the pen so that the dog is less inclined to circle. Walk backwards around the pen, gradually moving away from the fence and walking in smaller circles. Then gradually try walking straight backwards. Once the fetch is mastered, you are ready for the outrun.

Outrun: To teach the outrun, begin near the sheep with the dog by your side in the *down* position, then give a flanking command in an excited voice. If the dog runs directly to the sheep, run alongside it, forcing it outward. Ideally, the dog should follow a pear-shaped pathway around to the opposite side of the sheep, staying far enough away from the sheep that they do not react. As the dog seems to catch on, gradually back up from the sheep so that the outrun is longer. Eventually, your Aussie should be able to do outruns of 200 to 400 yards (183 to 366 m).

Drive: The drive is essentially the opposite of the fetch, and many dogs have difficulty with it at first because it involves pushing stock away from the handler rather than toward the handler. The best place to teach the drive is on a dirt road with fences on both sides, but you can improvise a lane with portable construction fencing. With the stock in the lane, place

Top: Controlling a herd of cattle is grueling work. Middle: Rounding up a runaway. Bottom: Penning requires finesse.

The correct course of the outrun.

the dog tries to get around the side of the stock, *down* it and give the stock a chance to move on before again giving the "*Walk up*" command. This change in direction will confuse many dogs, but eventually your Aussie will get the idea of staying between you and the stock.

Shed: The shed is one of the most difficult, but useful and impressive, of the herding dog's talents. In it, one animal is singled out from the group and kept away from it. To teach it, the herd should be somewhat strung out. The handler then forces a break in the line of animals, causing one animal to become separated. You can also force that break by calling your dog to you

the dog between you and the stock. Give the command "*Walk up*." Many dogs will attempt to get to the opposite side of the stock so they can move it toward you. If the lane is narrow enough, this will be extremely difficult for the dog to do without causing the sheep to move forward, away from both dog and handler. If

Training to shed stock from the herd.

through the herd. The herding dog's instinctive reaction is to gather that animal back into the herd, but you must tell it "*This one!*" and then "*Walk up,*" encouraging the dog to approach the single animal. This will take plenty of patience but eventually your Aussie will learn to turn the single animal from the group and hold it there.

Penning: Penning sheep is another task that seems difficult at first. Start by having your Aussie hold sheep to you as you stand alongside a fence. By moving slightly you can cause the sheep to start to bolt in one direction, and your Aussie can practice anticipating their movement and holding them to you. Then stand by a gate and open it toward you, allowing the sheep to go through. *Down* your dog before it can follow them through. In this way it comes to know that you wanted the sheep behind the fence and that it shouldn't rush in and gather them back to you. When your dog is adept at this step, you can set up a gate with only a couple of fence panels on either side, and finally, set up a pen in the middle of the practice area.

Teamwork

Whether training your Aussie for work on the ranch, herding trials, or simply mutual enjoyment, you, too, will most likely find yourself driven. Not only is herding good mental and physical exercise for your Aussie, but the teamwork involved is a wonderful bonding experience. No wonder so many Aussie owners eventually move to the country and find themselves surrounded by sheep!

Herding Terms

✔ **Approach:** how the dog comes toward the stock.

✔ **Balance:** position of the dog that allows it to control the movements of the stock.

✔ **Close-running:** working very near to the stock.

✔ **Crook:** shepherd's staff with a hook on one end.

✔ **Cross-drive:** moving the stock at a right angle to the handler.

✔ **Drive:** move the stock away from the handler.

✔ **Eye:** intense stare by the dog, often while creeping toward the stock.

✔ **Fetch:** bring the stock toward the handler.

✔ **Flanks:** commands telling the dog which direction to circle around the stock.

✔ **Gather:** collect dispersed stock into a compact group.

✔ **Grip:** bite the stock.

✔ **Head:** move in front of the stock to stop its forward progress.

✔ **Heel:** move sheep from behind, usually by heel nipping.

✔ **Lift:** point at which the dog first moves the sheep forward.

✔ **Outrun:** act of running from the handler and around the sheep to their far side.

✔ **Pen:** small enclosure into which stock are driven.

✔ **Shed:** separate one specific animal from the herd.

✔ **Wear:** move the stock toward the handler; also, side-to-side movements of the dog in an effort to group stock.

ACTIVITIES WITH YOUR AUSTRALIAN SHEPHERD

It's impossible to own an Aussie without becoming enthralled by the beauty of it deftly controlling a herd of sheep, having your breath taken away by its dazzling agility, or being overwhelmed by its intelligence or the striking picture it makes standing in the field. It's only natural to want to show off the apple of your eye. Proud owners have flaunted their Aussies in herding trials for many years, and more recently have added dog shows, obedience trials, agility competitions, and a bevy of other competitive venues. Aussies have in turn proven to be formidable competitors.

Herding Competitions

Although the true value of a herding dog lies in what it can do on the ranch, many Aussie owners also find enjoyment in herding tests and trials. Tests generally refer to noncompetitive events in which dogs must exhibit a certain level of proficiency to pass; trials usually denote competitive events in which dogs are scored and placed in relation to one another. Several organizations sponsor tests and trials; although the general requirements are similar, each has slight differences, so you should obtain the official rules from each organization.

With all the activities awaiting you and your Aussie, your Aussie may need an understudy just to get some rest!

The following titles are offered by the different organizations sponsoring herding tests or trials. (Note: Several titles are seen in conjunction with the lowercase letter s, c, or d. This denotes that the title was earned with either sheep, cattle, or ducks.)

Australian Shepherd Club of America (ASCA)

✔ *Started Trial Dog (STD), Open Trial Dog (OTD),* and *Advanced Trial Dog (ATD)* represent progressively more demanding trial titles. The *Working Trial Championship (WTCh)* is awarded when the ATD is earned with all three eligible stock species (sheep, cattle, and ducks).

✔ *Post-Advanced Trial Dog (PATD)* requires working stock in a large field.

✔ *Ranch Trial Dog (RTD)* is awarded based on performance with sheep, goats, or cattle in a ranch setting. It includes pen work, sorting work, chute work, and pasture work, in which the pasture is at least 5 acres.

✔ *Ranch Dog certification (RD)* is earned with the dog being judged working stock at home. The dog must regularly work stock as an aid to its owner's livelihood. More advanced certifications of Ranch Dog Good (RDG) and Ranch Dog Excellent (RDX) are also awarded. Request the free Stockdog Rulebook from the ASCA for more detailed information (see page 109 for address).

American Kennel Club (AKC)

✔ *Herding Test (HT)* and *Pre-Trial (PT)* are noncompetitive titles based on the display of basic herding instinct and ability.

✔ *Herding Started (HS), Herding Intermediate (HI)*, and *Herding Excellent (HX)* represent progressively more demanding titles. Three qualifying scores are required for each title.

✔ *Herding Championships (HCh)* are earned by earning placements in the most advanced level after completing the HX title.

Three types of courses are available: The "A" course requires working stock through obstacles and penning within an arena; the "B" course requires an outrun, lift, fetch, pen, and, for an HX, a shed. The "C" course is performed with larger flocks in more open areas.

Request the herding tests and trials rulebook from the AKC for more detailed information (see page 109 for address).

American Herding Breed Association (AHBA)

Tests:

✔ *Herding Capability Test (HCT)* consists of a test of basic instinct and of basic stock-moving abilities.

✔ *Junior Herding Dog Test (JHD)* consists of a simple course ending in a fence-line pen.

To earn these titles requires two qualifying scores using either sheep, goats, ducks, geese, or sometimes cattle.

Trials:

✔ *Herding Trial Dog trials (HTD)* include three successively more difficult levels (I, II, III), all of which include an outrun, lift, fetch, drive, and pen.

✔ *Herding Ranch Dog trials (HRD)* include a greater variety of elements and tasks more like what a working stock dog might actually encounter.

To earn these titles requires two qualifying scores using either sheep, goats, ducks (except for HRD), geese, or cattle. A small initial following the title signifies which species that title represents.

✔ *Herding Trial Championship (HTCh)* is awarded after earning ten additional qualifying scores after completing the HTD III or HRD III title.

Obedience Trials

Like all good herding dogs, the Aussie is intelligent and amenable to directions, the two main ingredients of a standout obedience dog. If you don't have access to livestock, you can still exercise your Aussie's mind by training it for competitive obedience. Several organizations, including the ASCA, AKC, and United Kennel Club (UKC), sponsor obedience trials, with progressively more difficult levels. The UKC trials include a few more difficult exercises; the ASCA and AKC trials are similar. The lowest level of AKC or ASCA Companion Dog (CD) requires the dog to:

✔ heel on lead, sitting automatically each time you stop, negotiating right, left, and about turns without guidance from you, and changing to a faster and slower pace.

✔ heel in a figure 8 around two people, still on lead.

✔ stand still off lead 6 feet (1.8 m) away from you and allow a judge to touch it.

✔ do the exercises in number 1, except off lead.

✔ come to you when called from 20 feet (6.1 m) away, and then return to *heel* position on command.

✔ stay in a sitting position with a group of other dogs, while you are 20 feet (6.1 m) away, for one minute.

✔ stay in a *down* position with the same group, while you are 20 feet (6.1 m) away, for three minutes.

Higher degrees of Companion Dog Excellent (CDX), or Utility Dog (UD) and Utility Dog Excellent (UDX), are a lot more fun and include retrieving, jumping, and hand signal and scent discrimination exercises. Child's play for an Aussie! The supreme obedience title is the Obedience Trial Champion (OTCH), awarded only to dogs with UDs that outscore many other UD dogs in many, many trials. Very few dogs of any breeds have earned the OTCH degree, but Aussies are among them.

Dog obedience classes are often sponsored by obedience clubs, and are a must if you plan to compete. They are a valuable source of training advice and encouragement from people who are experienced obedience competitors.

If you enter competition with your Aussie, remember this as your Golden Rule: Companion Dog means just that; being upset at your dog because it made a mistake defeats the purpose of obedience as a way of promoting a harmonious partnership between trainer and dog. Failing a trial, in the scope of life, is an insignificant event. Never let a ribbon or a few points become more important than a trusting relationship with your companion. Besides, your Aussie will forgive you for the times you mess up!

Tracking Trials

If you enjoy spending misty mornings in the field with your Aussie, you might enjoy tracking.

Begin training by walking a simple path and dropping little treats along it. The dog will soon learn that the treats can be discovered simply by following your trail. If your Aussie can't bear to be parted from you, you can also begin training by hiding from it and then allowing it to sniff its way to you. Of course, the actual tracking tests will require considerably more training than this!

A dog can earn the Tracking Dog (TD) title by following a 440- to 500-yard (402- to 457-m) track with three to five turns laid from 30 minutes to 2 hours before. A Tracking Dog Excellent (TDX) title is earned by following an "older" (three to five hours) and longer (800- to 1,000-yard [732- to 914-m]) track with five to seven turns, with some more challenging circumstances. One of these circumstances is the existence of cross tracks laid by another tracklayer about 1½ hours after the first track was laid. In addition, the actual track may cross various types of terrain and obstacles, including plowed land, woods, streams, bridges, and lightly traveled roads.

Aussie Sense: Olfaction

The Australian Shepherd, like all dogs, has a powerful sense of smell. The Aussie's scenting ability is so vastly superior to ours that it is as though we were blind in comparison. No machine has been developed that can outperform the dog's nose in olfactory detection. Some evidence exists that dogs with more olfactory area, which corresponds to a long, deep muzzle, have better scenting powers, but this has never been proven. Certainly, Aussies have proven themselves on the trail, and are especially adept at jobs requiring them to search out hidden people and contraband.

Weaving around poles at full speed is part of an agility course. Notice the A-frame and tunnel in the background.

A dog can earn the Variable Surface Tracking (VST) title by following a three- to five-hour track, 600 to 800 yards (549 to 732 m) long, over a variety of surfaces such as might be normally encountered when tracking in the real world. At least three different surface areas are included, of which at least one must include vegetation and at least two must be devoid of vegetation (for example, sand or concrete). Tracks may even go through buildings, and may be crossed by animal, pedestrian, or vehicular traffic. Aussies may not have been bred to use their noses, but they have nonetheless proven themselves more than competent at it.

Agility Trials

Aussies can jump, sprint, climb, balance, and weave with amazing nimbleness, and the sport of agility allows them to hone their skills on an obstacle course. Among the obstacles are open and closed tunnels, elevated walk-over, A-frame, seesaws, weave poles, pause table, and several types of jumps. The Aussie has almost an unfair advantage at this sport! The AKC awards, in increasing level of difficulty, the titles Novice Agility Dog (NAD), Open Agility Dog (CAD), Agility Dog Excellent (ADE), and Master Agility Excellent (MAX). The ASCA offers three different class types: Regular, which requires all the obstacles to be cleared in a set time; Gamblers, which is a faster-paced class that also requires the dog to work on its own; and Jumpers, which is a fast-paced competition of jumping. Several levels within the classes are offered, and the ASCA offers a plethora of titles. The United States Dog Agility Association (USDAA) and United Kennel Club (UKC) also sponsor trials and award titles.

Many obedience clubs are now sponsoring agility training, but you can start some of the fundamentals at home. Entice your dog to walk through a tunnel made of sheets draped over chairs; guide it with treats to weave in and out

Climbing the A-frame.

In the ring, a top winning Aussie keeps his attention on his handler despite all the distractions.

of a series of poles made from several plumber's helpers placed in line. Make it comfortable walking on a wide, raised board. Teach it to jump through a tire and over a hurdle. If you can't find a club to train with, you can make your own equipment. Contact the AKC, ASCA, USDAA, or UKC for regulations. Agility is the fastest-growing dog sport in America, and Aussies are among the best at it.

Conformation Shows

The Aussie's build reflects its athletic heritage, and conformation shows judge how well each dog conforms to the physical standard of perfection. As long as your Aussie doesn't have any disqualifying traits (including having been spayed, neutered, lacking two normally descended testicles in males, or other problems described on page 108), it is eligible to compete.

Aussies also compete in Frisbee catching contests. A soft flying disk is the best for training.

Training for showing is fairly easy. The show Aussie must trot easily about the ring and pose when stopped, and allow a judge to touch it all over without showing resentment or shyness. It helps if your Aussie will "bait," that is, look attentively at a little tidbit or toy. Many local kennel clubs offer handling classes and practice matches. Professional handlers can show your dog for you and probably win more often than you would, but there is nothing like the thrill of winning when you are on the other end of the lead!

At an AKC or ASCA show, each time a judge chooses your dog as the best dog of its sex that is not already a Champion it wins up to five points, depending on how many dogs it defeats. To become an AKC Champion (Ch) your Aussie must win fifteen points including two majors (defeating enough dogs to win three to five points at a time); an ASCA championship requires fifteen points and three majors.

For the Record. . .

✔ The ASCA Supreme WTCh is awarded to Aussies that win Champion cattle, sheep, and ducks at the same trial—a feat accomplished by only three dogs: WTCh Slash Slide Me Sweet, CD, and the brothers WTCh The Bull of Twin Oaks CD, RDX, RTD-cs and WTCh Twin Oaks Kit Carson RDX, RTD-cs. Kit Carson is top-winning herding Aussie of all time, winning an amazing 13 ASCA Finals Championships.

✔ Nearly 100 Aussies have earned the ASCA UD title, but only a few dogs of any breed can boast of multiple generations of Utility Dogs. U-UD Riptide's Moonlight AKC/ASCA UD is a sixth generation UD titlest! Her uncle, U-UD Riptide Simon Says AKC/ASCA UD, AD, FDCH, VAD, NA, NAC-V, NJC-V, NGC-V, HC, TT, CGC is a fifth generation UD titlest (and the first AKC UD Aussie) that also boasts agility and flyball titles!

✔ The first ASCA TDX was Arrowhead's Homeward Bound CD, TDX; he won his title at the astounding age of only 9½ months.

✔ After eating snail bait as a puppy, "Haley" was abandoned by her owners at the veterinary clinic. Upon recovering, her adoptive owner trained her in agility, where she became Scotswood's Haley's Comet, ADCH, NATCH, O-NATCH, MAD, RM, SM, EAC, EJC, EGC, winner of the 1995 North American Dog Agility Council's "20" Elite Championship, and one of only four dogs elected to represent the United States in the 1994 World Cup in agility held in Switzerland! Not to be outdone, Ahlarlay's

Kodiak Scamp, CD, STDsdc, AATCH, MAD, NATCH is the first dog to become an ASCA Agility Trial Champion.

✔ The ASCA awards the Versatility Champion (VCH) and Supreme Versatility Champion (SVCH) to dogs that have earned titles in conformation, obedience, and herding. One of the breed's most versatile and titled Aussies is the amazing SVCH WTCH ASCA/AKC/CKC Ch Beauwood's Rustlin in the Sun ASCA/AKC UDT, RD, HI, RV-N, CKC CD, HTDs, TT, CGC.

✔ The all-time AKC Best in Show winner, Am Can Ch Bayshore's Flapjack, not only won an amazing 27 Best in Shows, but twice won the National Specialty, plus 175 Herding Groups. His winning genes are reflected in his over 40 Champion offspring.

✔ Perhaps the most watched Aussie ever was Hyper Hank, who was invited to perform his amazing Frisbee feats during half-time of Super Bowl XII.

✔ A true Aussie hero was a Search and Rescue dog aptly named Ranger (officially Sierra Charm's Mountain Ranger). Ranger was certified in Wilderness, Water, Cadaver, Evidence and Basic Urban Disaster searches, and was sent on over 100 missions. In his career he saved four lives, located three bodies, found a murder weapon, and helped locate a kidnapped child. One of his most memorable finds was a hiker near death who had been lost in the mountains for six days. Ranger was tragically killed in the line of duty, and was buried in a place of honor with 200 people in attendance. As one searcher said: "God must have had one serious search up there; he called the best to help . . . ."

Community Service

Aussies are one of the most versatile breeds when it comes to competing successfully in a variety of fields. Some Aussies do even more, however, and win the hearts of those whose lives they touch.

Search and Rescue

Dogs have been used for finding lost people for decades, but only recently have groups of committed dog owners joined together to train their dogs to be ready to save a life. These dogs are available for local emergencies, and may also be prepared to fly across the country in the cases of disasters. They may search miles of wilderness for a lost child or tons of rubble for a buried victim. Whereas so many dog training activities seem to have little relevance in society, search and rescue is the exception. Your long hours of training just may save a life. Search-and-rescue dogs are the cream of the crop. If your Aussie is capable of competing in obedience, agility, and tracking, it has the basics of a search-and-rescue (SAR) dog. But an SAR Aussie is much more. These dogs must respond reliably to commands, negotiate precarious footing, follow a trail and locate articles, and, most of all, use air scenting to pinpoint the location of a hidden person. Well-trained dogs can locate a person from a quarter of a mile away, or buried under snow, rubble, or even under water. Tall order, no doubt, but one that several heroic Aussies—and their equally heroic handlers—have already filled. An SAR dog is only half of the team; handlers must also be trained. Together the development of an SAR team requires many hours of committed work, hours made worthwhile by grateful tears and saved lives.

Therapy

Aussies excel at many roles, but perhaps one of the most important is that of canine therapist. As more of the population becomes elderly and either unable to care for or keep a pet, the result is particularly sad for lonely people who may have relied on the comfort and companionship of a pet throughout most of their independent years. Studies have shown that pet ownership increases life expectancy and petting animals can lower blood pressure. In recent years nursing home residents have come to look forward to visits by dogs, including many Aussies. These dogs must be meticulously well mannered and well groomed; to be registered as a Certified Therapy Dog a dog must demonstrate that it will act in an obedient, outgoing, gentle manner to strangers. The Aussie combines the perfect blend of attributes for this most vital job: they are outgoing but tractable, and just right for a big hug. They can entertain children and adults alike with their endless ability to perform feats of intelligence. They seem to be in tune with what a particular person most needs, giving a gentle nuzzle to the unsure and a big smile to those in need of cheering up. If you've ever wondered how you could make a difference, consider having your Aussie bring a smile to someone's life.

Service Dogs

Several Aussies have devoted their lives to helping disabled people. Aussies have proven themselves as capable guide dogs for the blind, hearing dogs for the deaf, and all-purpose assistants for the physically challenged. These are not part-time jobs, but you can still lend a hand by being a puppy home for Aussies that may one day open the world to others.

Most Aussie owners exercise their dogs not by herding, agility, or other organized activities but by sharing time together on a walk or run. With the move of many Aussies to more urban areas, special precautions need to be taken for the safety of your dog. Aussies are smart and obedient dogs, but even they can act unpredictably when the unpredictable occurs. Another dog may attack, or a cat may run underfoot, or the chance to exercise that herding instinct may arise; whatever the reason, the trustworthy dog forgets itself for just a moment—and that's all it takes to run in front of a car. Trust is wonderful, but careless or blind trust is deadly.

Protecting Your Pet

1. Never allow your Aussie to run loose near traffic.

2. Never unhook the leash until you know everything about the area.

3. Watch for poisonous snakes, alligators, or other animals that could attack your dog.

4. Watch for small animals and dogs that your dog could chase.

5. Look out for cliffs, roadways, and drainage culverts.

6. Avoid wilderness areas during hunting season.

A well-trained and conditioned Aussie is the best hiking partner you could ask for.

Walking and Jogging

Walking the dog on lead is an excellent low-impact exercise for both of you, and is especially good for elderly or recovering dogs. If you pick a regular time of day for your walk you will have your own personal fitness coach goading you off the couch like clockwork. For a walk around the neighborhood, use a choke or martingale collar so that it cannot slip over your Aussie's head, a 6-foot (1.8-m) non-chain leash, or a retractable leash. Retractable leashes are great for walks, but you must be especially vigilant when using them because dogs can still dart out into the path of traffic when on them. Keep an eye out for loose dogs and cats, and hold your dog close around stray animals and passing pedestrians.

Keep up a brisk pace, and gradually work up to longer distances. An Aussie should walk at the very least a mile (1.6 km) daily, and would prefer to walk several miles. Jogging can also be fun for your Aussie, but you must work up to longer distances gradually and avoid hot weather. Dogs can't cool themselves as well as humans can, and heatstroke in jogging dogs has taken the lives of far too many. Check the footpads regularly for abrasions, gravel, tearing, or blistering from hot pavement. In winter, check between the pads for balls of ice, and rinse the feet when returning from walking on rock salt. Finally, never jog, jump, or overexert a puppy. Their bones can be overstressed and damaged. Let a pup run until it's tired, but no more.

Although it's tempting to be lazy and jog your dog beside a bicycle or car, these are risky practices. It's too easy for your dog to see a cat or squirrel and either pull you over or run into your path. If you do elect to try the lazy way out, despite warnings, you must train your dog to understand "*heel*" before starting, and have your dog in *heel* position (except farther out from you) when on the move.

Aussies need exercise, but it must be safe exercise. Do your best to give them this chance, but as the sensible half of the partnership, don't take chances when it comes to safety. Besides, whether walking, jogging, or running, your Aussie will relish most the chance to simply share any adventure, no matter how wild or sedate, with its favorite person—you!

Finding a Lost Dog

Aussies usually stick pretty close to home, but sometimes the unforeseeable happens and you and your dog are suddenly separated. If so, you need to act quickly. Don't rely on the dog's fabled ability to find its way home—yours may not be gifted in this area.

Start your search at the very worst place you could imagine your dog, usually the nearest road, but don't drive so recklessly that you endanger your own dog's life should it run across the road. Next, get pictures of your dog and go door to door. Call the local animal control, police department, and veterinarians. Make up large posters with a picture of your dog or a similar-looking Aussie. Take out an ad in the local paper. Mention a reward, but do not specify an amount.

Dognappers

The striking look and popular perception of the Aussie could make it attractive to dognappers. Never leave your dog in a place where it could be taken. Some dognappers steal dogs so they can collect large rewards, but you should never give anyone reward money before seeing your dog. Some scam artists answer lost dog ads and ask for money to ship the dog back to you from a distance or to pay veterinarian bills, when they don't really have your dog. If your dog is tattooed, you can have the person read the tattoo to you in order to positively identify it.

Identification

Even license tags cannot always ensure your dog's return, because they must be on the dog to be effective. Tattooing your Social Security number or your dog's registration number on the inside of its thigh provides a permanent means of identification; these numbers can be registered with one of the several lost pet recovery agencies. Microchips are available that are placed under the dog's skin with a simple injection. They contain information about the dog and cannot be removed, but require a special scanner (owned by most animal shelters) to be read. You may wish to discuss this option with your veterinarian or local breeders. The best solution is all three: license tag, tattoo, and microchip; of course, the best solution is to never chance getting separated from your companion.

Travel

Aussies make excellent travel companions. A dog gives you a good excuse to stop and enjoy the scenery up close, and maybe even get some exercise along the way. With proper planning, you will find that an Aussie copilot can steer you to destinations you might otherwise have passed.

Without proper planning, sharing your trip with any dog can be a nightmare, as you are turned away from motels, parks, attractions, and beaches. It's no fun trying to sneak a dog into a motel room (Aussies are just a tad too big to fit under your coat; besides, even the mutest Aussie will find plenty to bark at once it discovers you're trying to keep it quiet!). Several books are available listing establishments that accept pets. Call ahead to attractions to see if they have safe boarding arrangements for pets.

The number of establishments that accept pets decreases yearly. You can thank dog owners who seem to think their little Poopsie is above the law, owners who let Poopsie poop on sidewalks, beaches, and playgrounds, bark herself hoarse in the motel room, and leave behind wet spots on the carpet and chew marks on the chairs. Miraculously, there still remain some places where pets are welcome. Please do everything you can to convince motel managers that dogs can be civilized guests.

Whether you will be spending your nights at a motel, campground, or even a friend's home, always have your dog on its very best behavior. Ask beforehand if it will be OK for you to bring your Aussie. Have your dog clean and parasite-free. Do not allow your dog to run helter-skelter through the homes of friends. Bring your dog's own clean blanket or bed, or better yet, its cage. Your Aussie will appreciate the familiar place to sleep, and your friends and motel owners will breathe sighs of relief. Even though your dog may be accustomed to sleeping on furniture at home, a proper canine guest stays off the furniture when visiting. Walk your dog (and

Items to Pack for Traveling
✔ Heartworm preventive and any other medications, especially antidiarrhea medication
✔ Food and water bowls
✔ Food, dog biscuits, and chewies
✔ Bottled water or water from home; many dogs are very sensitive to changes in water and can develop diarrhea
✔ Flea comb and brush
✔ Moist towelettes, paper towels, and self-rinse shampoo
✔ Bedding
✔ Short and long leashes
✔ Sweater for cold weather
✔ Flashlight for night walks
✔ Plastic baggies or other items for poop disposal
✔ License tags, including a tag indicating where you could be reached while on your trip, or including the address of someone you know will be at home
✔ Health and rabies certificates
✔ Recent color photo in case your Aussie somehow gets lost

clean up after it) to make sure no accidents occur inside. If they do, clean them immediately—don't leave any surprises for your hosts! Changes in water or food, or simply stress, can often result in diarrhea, so be particularly attentive to taking your dog out often.

Never leave your dog unattended in a strange place. The dog's perception is that you have left and forgotten it; it either barks, tries to dig its way out through the doors and windows, or becomes upset and relieves itself on the carpet. Remember that anyone who allows your dog to spend the night is doing so with a certain amount of trepidation.

Car Travel

When in the car your Aussie will want to cuddle in your lap or close by your side, or hang its head out the window for a big whiff of country air. But you are smarter than your Aussie (at least in this matter) and know that it should always ride with the equivalent of a doggy seat belt: the cage. Not only can a cage help prevent accidents by keeping your dog from using your lap as a trampoline, but if there is an accident, a cage can save your dog's life. A cage with a padlocked door can also be useful when you need to leave the dog in the car with the windows down.

Always walk your Aussie on lead when away from home. If frightened or distracted, your dog could become disoriented and lost. The long retractable leads are wonderful for traveling. Keep an eye out for little nature excursions, which are wonderful for refreshing both dog and owner. But always do so with a cautious eye; never risk your or your dog's safety by stopping in totally desolate locales.

A vacation day at the beach—first make sure that dogs are allowed, then keep your Aussie on its best behavior.

Air Travel

Air travel with your pet is fairly safe, but should not be undertaken frivolously. Although air compartments are heated, they are not air-conditioned, and in hot weather dogs have been known to overheat while the plane was still on the runway. Never ship in the heat of day. It's best if your dog can fly as excess baggage, but if you must ship it by itself, it is usually better to ship "counter to counter" than to ship as air freight. Make sure the cage is secure, and for good measure put an elastic "bungee" band around the cage door. Don't feed your dog before traveling. The night before the trip, fill a small bucket with water and freeze it. Take it out of the cooler just before the flight and attach it to the inside of the cage door with an eyebolt snap; as it melts during the flight the dog will have water that

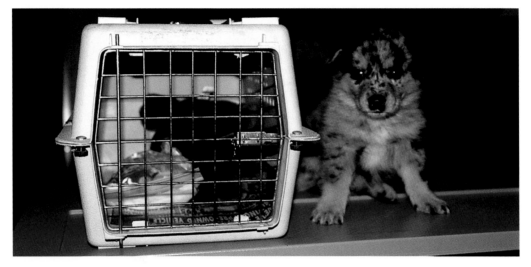

All packed up and somewhere to go—a new home!

otherwise might have spilled out during the loading process. Also include a large chewbone to occupy your jet-setter. Be sure to line the cage with soft, absorbent material, preferably something that can be thrown away if soiled.

Boarding

Sometimes you must leave your dog behind when you travel. Your dog may be more comfortable if an experienced pet-sitter or responsible friend comes to your home and feeds and exercises it regularly. This works best if you have a doggy door.

Your Aussie may be safer (if not quite as contented) if you board it at a kennel. The ideal kennel will be approved by the American Boarding Kennel Association, have climate-controlled accommodations, and will keep your Aussie either indoors or in a combination indoor/outdoor run. Make an unannounced

visit to the kennel and ask to see the facilities. While you can't expect spotlessness and a perfumed atmosphere, most runs should be clean and the odor should not be overwhelming. All dogs should have clean water and at least some dogs should have soft bedding. A solid divider should prevent dogs in adjoining runs from direct contact with one another. Strange dogs should not be allowed to mingle. Outside runs should be surrounded by a tall fence for extra security. Good kennels will require proof of immunizations, and an incoming check for fleas. They will allow you to bring toys and bedding, and will administer prescribed medication. They will have arrangements for emergency veterinary care.

Whatever means you choose, always leave emergency numbers and your veterinarian's name. Make arrangements with your veterinarian to treat your dog for any problems that may arise. This means leaving a written agreement stating that you give permission for treatment and accept responsibility for charges.

Limping may or may not indicate a serious problem. *Mild* lameness should be treated by complete rest; if it still persists after three days your dog will need to be examined by its veterinarian. Ice packs may help minimize swelling if applied immediately after an injury. Aspirin or other prescription medications may alleviate some of the discomfort of injuries, but never give them if your dog is on its way to surgery. If you administer pain medication, you must confine your dog; lack of pain could encourage it to use the injured limb, ultimately resulting in further injury.

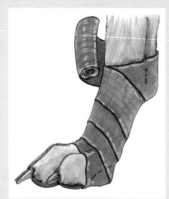

One method of wrapping an injured foot is to begin near the toes with the Vet-Wrap wrapping around the leg at a 45 degree angle to the ground so that it crosses over itself and clings better. Use a strip of adhesive tape to anchor its position at the top and bottom.

Fractures

Any time a dog is lame and also exhibits swelling or deformation of the affected leg, extreme pain, or grinding or popping sounds, it could indicate a break or another serious problem. It is imperative that the fractured area not be further traumatized by attempts to immobilize it; if in doubt, leave it alone and seek veterinary attention.

Feet and Toes

1. If a toe is swollen, does not match its fellow on the opposite foot in shape and position, or makes a grinding sound when moved, or if the dog is in considerable pain, the toe should be immobilized and checked by your veterinarian. Meanwhile, minimize swelling by applying cold packs or placing the foot in a bucket of cold water.

2. Examine the feet of a lame dog for burrs, cuts, peeled pads, or misaligned toes. Split or broken nails can be treated by cutting the nail as short as possible and soaking it in warm salt water. Apply an antibiotic and then a human fingernail mender, followed by a bandage.

3. Cuts and peeled pads should be carefully flushed with warm water, and an antibacterial ointment applied. Cover the area with gauze, then wrap the foot with Vet-Wrap (a stretchable bandage that clings to itself). You can also add padding. Change the dressing twice daily (or any time it gets wet) and restrict exercise until it heals. If you need a quick fix for a minor injury, you can fashion a makeshift pad by adhering a thin piece of rubber or leather to the bottom of the pad with Super-Glue, or you can apply a coat of Nu-Skin (available at drugstores) if the injury is not too extensive. Peeled pads are very painful. A local anesthetic such as nonsteroidal hemorrhoid cream or a topical toothache salve can help ease some of the discomfort. Deep cuts or extensive peeling should be checked by your veterinarian.

4. If the webbing between the toes is split, it will continue to split further. Have the condition checked by your veterinarian.

5. A deep cut directly above and behind the foot may sever the ligaments to the toes, causing them to lose their arch. Immediate veterinary attention should be sought.

6. A "jammed toe" results from the stubbing of a toe on a root, rock, or other hard surface. A toe that is simply bruised will improve with rest, but any toe injury is potentially serious.

7. A displaced toe will stick out to the side and the dog will be in extreme pain. Pull the toe gently forward and allow it to go back into its proper position. Wrap the foot in Vet-Wrap and seek veterinary attention. Toes that become dislocated often have stretched or torn ligaments, and the problem will tend to recur and worsen with each subsequent dislocation. An extended rest is mandatory. Keeping the nail of the affected toe trimmed as short as possible may help, as will wrapping the foot in Vet-Wrap before running and avoiding running on hard surfaces.

Knee Injuries

Knee injuries, especially of the cruciate ligaments, are common in dogs, especially overweight dogs. They can also arise when the dog is pushed sideways while running. Most cruciate tears do not mend on their own; still, cruciate surgery requires a commitment to careful nursing and should not be undertaken casually.

Muscle Injuries

The most common non-foot injuries are muscle injuries. These usually cause little lameness but pronounced swelling, or can be felt as an indentation in a muscle. Torn muscles may need surgery for a complete recovery. All muscle injuries should be treated with an initial ice pack followed by at least a week's rest.

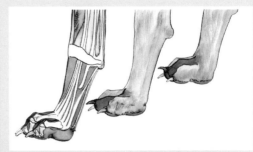

Normal toe placement, a dropped toe (due to tearing of the superficial digital flexor tendon), and a knocked up toe (due to tearing of the deep digital flexor tendon). These tendons are located in the rear of the pastern or hock.

Puppy Problems

Puppies are especially susceptible to bone and joint injuries, and should never be allowed to jump from high places or run until exhausted. Persistent limping in puppies may result from one of several developmental bone problems, and should be checked by the veterinarian. Both puppies and adults should be discouraged from romping on slippery floors that could cause them to lose their footing.

Older Dogs

In older dogs, or dogs with a previous injury, limping is often the result of osteoarthritis. Arthritis can be treated with aspirin, but should be done so only under veterinary supervision. Do not use naxopren. Your veterinarian can prescribe drugs that may help greatly. Any time a young or middle-aged dog shows signs of arthritis, especially in a joint that has not been previously injured, it should be examined by its veterinarian.

THE OLDER AUSSIE

You and your Aussie have a lifetime of experiences to share. Your life may change dramatically in the years to come: marriage, divorce, new baby, new home—for better or worse your Aussie will still depend on you and still love you. Always remember the promise you made to yourself and your future puppy before you made the commitment to share your life: to keep your interest in your dog and care for it every day of its life with as much love and enthusiasm as you did the first day it arrived home.

Changes in Your Aussie

Remember, too, that your Aussie will change through the years. The Aussie's high energy and natural athleticism sometimes mislead owners into forgetting that Aussies, like all dogs, get old. One day you will look at your youngster and be shocked to discover its face has silvered and its gait has stiffened. It sleeps longer and more soundly than it did as a youngster, and is slower to get going. It may be less eager to play and more content to lie in the sun. Getting your dog to healthy old age is a worthy accomplishment. Just make sure that you appreciate all the stages along the way.

Every stage of an Aussie's life is its best. Puppies are so full of curiosity and mischief,

The journey from puppyhood to old age is gradual but still far too fast.

adolescents begin to blossom into adults, and adults mature into true dependable companions. Anyone who has had an Aussie for its entire life, however, would probably assert it is the senior Aussie that is the best. With the wisdom of years, the Aussie becomes almost human in its ability to tune into your emotions. The older Aussie, its eyes often hazy due to cataracts, its gait stiff, and its face gray, is, in the opinion of many Aussie fanciers, the most beautiful Aussie of all.

Living with an Older Aussie

It is important to keep your older Aussie relatively active. Both physical activity and metabolic rates decrease in older animals, meaning that they require fewer calories to maintain the same weight. Older dogs that continue being fed the same as when they were young risk becoming obese; such dogs have a greater risk of cardiovascular and joint problems.

While Aussies of any age enjoy a soft warm bed, it is an absolute necessity for older Aussies. Arthritis is a common cause of intermittent stiffness and lameness, and it can be helped with heat, a soft bed, moderate exercise, and possibly drug therapy.

Introduction of a new puppy or pet may be welcomed and encourage your dog to play, but if your dog is not used to other dogs, the newcomer will more likely be resented and be a

Ailments in Older Dogs

Ailment	Common Cause
✔ diarrhea	kidney or liver disease, pancreatitis
✔ coughing	heart disease, tracheal collapse, lung cancer
✔ difficulty eating	periodontal disease, oral tumors
✔ decreased appetite	kidney, liver, or heart disease, pancreatitis, cancer
✔ increased appetite	diabetes, Cushing's syndrome
✔ weight loss	heart, liver, or kidney disease, diabetes, cancer
✔ abdominal distention	heart or kidney disease, Cushing's syndrome, tumor
✔ increased urination	diabetes, kidney or liver disease, cystitis, Cushing's syndrome
✔ limping	arthritis, patellar luxation
✔ nasal discharge	tumor, periodontal disease

source of irritation. Some older dogs become cranky and less patient, especially when dealing with puppies or boisterous children. But don't just excuse behavioral changes, especially if they are sudden, as due simply to aging. They could be symptoms of pain or disease.

Long trips may be grueling, and boarding in a kennel may be extremely upsetting. The immune system may be less effective in older dogs, so it is increasingly important to shield your dog from infectious disease, chilling, overheating, and any stressful conditions.

Older dogs may experience hearing or visual loss. Be careful not to startle a dog with impaired senses, as a startled dog could snap in self-defense. The slight haziness that appears in the older dog's pupils is normal and has minimal effect upon vision, but some dogs, especially those with diabetes, may develop cataracts. These can be removed by a veterinary ophthalmologist if they are severe. Dogs with gradual vision loss can cope well as long as they are kept in familiar surroundings, and extra safety precautions are followed.

In general, any ailment that an older dog has

is magnified in severity compared to the same symptoms in a younger dog. Some of the more common symptoms and their possible cause in older Aussies are listed in the table above.

Vomiting and diarrhea in an old dog can signal many different problems; keep in mind that a small older dog cannot tolerate the dehydration that results from continued vomiting or diarrhea and you should not let it continue unchecked. The older dog should see its veterinarian at least twice a year. Blood tests can detect early stages of diseases that can benefit from treatment.

Older dogs present a somewhat greater anesthesia risk. Most of this increased risk can be negated, however, by first screening dogs with a complete medical workup.

Odor

Older dogs tend to have a stronger body odor, but don't just ignore increased odors. They could indicate specific problems, such as periodontal disease, impacted anal sacs, seborrhea, ear infections, or even kidney disease. Any strong odor should be checked by your veterinarian. Like people, dogs lose skin moisture as they age, and though dogs don't have to worry about wrinkles, their skin can become dry and itchy. Regular brushing can help by stimulating oil production.

Special Diets

Although some geriatric dogs are overweight, other Aussies lose weight and may need to eat puppy food in order to keep the pounds on. Most older dogs do not require a special diet unless they have a particular medical need for it (such as obesity: low calorie; kidney failure: low protein; heart failure: low sodium). Special diets should be prescribed by your veterinarian, and only after a thorough check of heart and kidney function.

Older dogs should be fed several small meals instead of one large meal, and should be fed on time. Moistening dry food or feeding canned food can help dogs with dental problems enjoy their meal. They may enjoy eating while lying down or eating from a raised platform.

Saying Farewell

If you are lucky enough to have an old Aussie, you still must accept that an end will come. Heart disease, kidney failure, and cancer eventually claim most of these senior citizens. Early detection can help delay their effects, but unfortunately can seldom prevent them ultimately.

Despite the best of care, a time will come when neither you nor your veterinarian can prevent your cherished pet from succumbing to old age or an incurable illness. It seems hard to believe that you will have to say good-bye

to someone who has been such a focal point of your life, a real member of your family.

You should realize that both of you have been fortunate to have shared so many good times, but make sure that your Aussie's remaining time is still pleasurable. Many terminal illnesses make your dog feel very ill, and there comes a point where your desire to keep your friend with you as long as possible may not be the kindest thing for either of you. If your dog no longer eats its dinner or treats, this is a sign that it does not feel well and you must face the prospect of doing what is best for your beloved friend.

Euthanasia is a difficult and personal decision that no one wishes to make, and that no one can make for you. Ask your veterinarian if there is a reasonable chance of your dog getting better, and if it is likely that your dog is suffering. Ask yourself if your dog is getting pleasure out of life, and if it enjoys most of its days. Financial considerations can be a factor if it means going into debt in exchange for just a little while longer. Your own emotional state must also be considered.

If you do decide that euthanasia is the kindest farewell gesture for your beloved friend, discuss with your veterinarian beforehand what will happen. Euthanasia is painless and involves giving an overdose of an anesthetic. If your dog is scared of the veterinary clinic, you might feel better having the doctor meet you at home or come out to your car. Although it won't be easy, try to remain with your dog so that its last moments will be filled with your love. Gather your memories of your Aussie and pen them in your heart forever. When it is time to let go, thank your Aussie for a job well done, and give it the final release.

That'll do.

Australian Shepherds in America are judged under two different but related standards of perfection. The ASCA, United Kennel Club, and Canadian Kennel Club use the ASCA standard, whereas the AKC uses the AKC standard. Both standards basically seek the same ideal, but may sometimes use slightly different wording. As the original standard, the ASCA standard is used here, with notations of any deviation from the AKC standard.

The ASCA Standard

General Appearance: The Australian Shepherd is a well-balanced dog of medium size and bone. He is attentive and animated, showing strength and stamina combined with unusual agility. Slightly longer than tall, he has a coat of moderate length and coarseness with coloring that offers variety and individuality in each specimen. An identifying characteristic is his natural or docked bobtail. In each sex, masculinity or femininity is well-defined.

AKC note: The AKC standard also makes note of the Aussie's strong herding and guarding instincts. It additionally describes the Aussie as lithe, and as being solid and muscular without cloddishness.

". . . solid and muscular without cloddishness"—AKC standard.

Character: The Australian Shepherd is intelligent, primarily a working dog of strong herding and guardian instincts. He is an exceptional companion. He is versatile and easily trained, performing his assigned tasks with great style and enthusiasm. He is reserved with strangers but does not exhibit shyness. Although an aggressive, authoritative worker, viciousness toward people or animals is intolerable.

AKC note: The AKC standard emphasizes that any display of shyness, fear, or aggression is to be severely penalized.

Head: Clean-cut, strong, dry, and in proportion to the body. The top skull is flat to slightly rounded, its length and width each equal to the length of the muzzle, which is in balance and proportioned to the rest if the head. The muzzle tapers slightly to a rounded tip. The stop is moderate but well-defined.

AKC note: The AKC standard states that the muzzle can be slightly shorter than the backskull. Viewed from the side, the topline of the backskull and muzzle form parallel planes divided by the stop. The backskull may show a slight occipital protuberance.

Teeth: A full complement of strong, white teeth meet in a scissors bite. An even bite is a fault. Teeth broken or missing by accident are not penalized. Disqualifications: Undershot bites; overshot bites exceeding one-eighth inch.

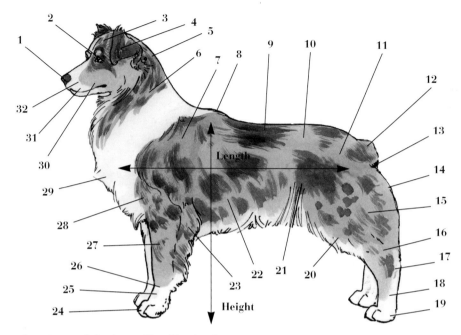

External anatomy of the Australian Shepherd.

1. nose	9. back	17. hock	25. forefoot
2. stop	10. loin	18. rear pastern	26. pastern
3. skull	11. rump (croup)	19. hindfoot	27. forearm
4. ear	12. tail	20. stifle	28. upper arm
5. crest	13. point of croup	21. flank	29. brisket
6. neck	14. hindquarters	22. chest	30. cheek
7. shoulder	15. upper thigh	23. elbow	31. flews
8. withers	16. lower thigh	24. paw	32. muzzle

AKC note: The AKC standard is more tolerant of a level (even) bite but prefers a scissors bite. It also points out that loss of contact of the upper and lower teeth caused by short center incisors in an otherwise correct mouth should not be considered undershot.

Eyes: Very expressive, showing attentiveness and intelligence. Clear, almond-shaped, and of moderate size, set a little obliquely, neither prominent nor sunken, with pupils dark, well-defined, and perfectly positioned. Color is brown, blue, amber, or any variation or combination including flecks and marbling.

AKC note: The AKC standard does not specify an oblique set, but adds that the expression should be alert and friendly.

Ears: Set on high at the side of the head, triangular and slightly rounded at the tip, of moderate size with length measured by bringing the tip of the ear around to the inner corner of the eye. The ears, at full attention, break slightly forward and over from one-quarter to one-half above the base. Prick ears and hound type ears are severe faults.

AKC note: The AKC standard does not mention a rounded tip and does not specify length.

Neck and Body: The neck is firm, clean, and in proportion to the body. It is of medium length and slightly arched at the crest, settling well into the shoulders. The body is firm and muscular. The topline appears level at a natural four-square stance. The chest is deep and strong with ribs well-sprung. The loin is strong and broad when viewed from the top. The bottom line carries well back with moderate tuck-up. The croup is moderately sloping, the ideal being 30 degrees from the horizontal. Tail is straight, not to exceed 4 inches, natural bobbed or docked.

AKC note: The AKC standard states that the chest should reach to the elbow.

Forequarters: The shoulder blades (scapulae) are long and flat, close set at the withers, approximately two fingers width at a natural stance, and are well laid back at an angle approximately 45 degrees to the ground. The upper arm (humerus) is attached at an approximate right angle to the shoulder line with forelegs dropping straight, perpendicular to the ground. The elbow joint is equidistant from the ground to the withers. The legs are straight and powerful. Pasterns are short, thick, and strong, but still flexible, showing a slight angle when viewed from the side. Feet are oval shaped, compact, with close-knit, well-arched toes. Pads are thick and resilient; nails short and strong. Dewclaws may be removed.

AKC note: The AKC standard specifies that the bone of the foreleg should be strong and oval rather than round.

Hindquarters: Width of hindquarters approximately equal the width of the forequarters at the shoulders. The angulation of the pelvis and the upper thigh (femur) corresponds to the angulation of the shoulder blade and upper arm forming an approximate right angle. Stifles are clearly defined, hock joints moderately bent. The metatarsi are short, perpendicular to the ground, and parallel to each other when viewed from the rear. Feet are oval shaped and compact with close-knit, well-arched toes. Pads are thick and resilient; nails short and strong. Rear dewclaws are removed.

Coat: Of medium texture, straight to slightly wavy, weather resistant, of moderate length with an undercoat. The quantity of undercoat varies with climate. Hair is short and smooth on the head, outside of ears, front of the forelegs, and below the hocks. Backs of the forelegs are moderately feathered; breeches are moderately full. There is a moderate mane and frill, more pronounced in dogs than bitches. Nontypical coats are severe faults.

Color: All colors are strong, clear, and rich. The recognized colors are blue merle, red (liver) merle, solid black, and solid red (liver), all with or without white markings and/or tan (copper) points with no order of preference. The blue merle and black have black pigmentation on the nose, lips, and eye-rims. Red and red merles have liver pigmentation on nose, lips, and eye-rims. Butterfly nose should not be faulted under one year of age. On all colors, the areas surrounding the ears and eyes are dominated by color other than white. The hairline of a white collar does not exceed the point of withers. Disqualifications: other than recognized colors, white body splashes, Dudley nose.

AKC note: The AKC standard more explicitly describes acceptable distribution of white areas. White is acceptable on the neck (but not to exceed the point of withers at the skin),

chest, legs, muzzle, underparts, blaze on head, and white extension from underpart up to 4 inches, measured from a horizontal line at the elbow. In addition, white body splashes are defined as white on the body between withers and tail, on the sides between elbows, and the back of hindquarters. It also states that in merles it is permissible to have small pink spots on the nose, but that these should not exceed 25 percent of the nose in adults.

Gait: Smooth, free, and easy; exhibiting agility of movement with a well-balanced, ground-covering stride. Fore and hind legs move straight and parallel with the center line of the body; as speed increases, the feet, both front and rear, converge toward the center line of gravity of the dog, while the topline remains firm and level.

The mane and frill are more pronounced in males than females.

AKC note: The AKC standard adds that the dog must be agile and able to change direction or alter gait instantly.

Size: Preferred height at the withers for males is 20 to 23 inches; that for females is 18 to 21 inches; however, quality is not to be sacrificed in favor of size. Disqualifications: Both ASCA and AKC disqualify male dogs that are lacking two normally descended testicles, in addition to those disqualifications mentioned within the body of the standard under color and teeth.

INFORMATION

Organizations

Australian Shepherd Club of
America
6091 East Highway 21
Bryan, TX 77803
(409) 778-1082

United States Australian
Shepherd Association
9330 N. County Road 15
Ft. Collins, CO 80524
(970) 568-3806

Aussie Rescue and Placement
Helpline
P.O. Box 85
Honesdale, PA 18431
(800) 892-ASCA

Second Time Around Aussie
Rescue
P.O. Box 722
Leona Valley, CA 93551
1-87-RESCUE US

American Kennel Club
260 Madison Avenue
New York, NY 10016
(212) 696-8200

AKC Registration and Information
5580 Centerview Drive, Ste. 200
Raleigh, NC 27606-3390
(919) 233-9767

Note: Many of these addresses
will change with periodic change
of officers. Current addresses can
usually be located through the
Internet.

Magazines

Aussie Times
Order through the ASCA

Australian Shepherd Journal
Order through the USASA

Dog World
500 N. Dearborn, Ste. 100
Chicago, IL 60610
(312) 396-0600

AKC Gazette
5580 Centerview Drive, Ste. 200
Raleigh, NC 27606-3390
(919) 233-9767

The Ranch Dog Trainer
Rt. 2, Box 333
West Plains, MO 65775

Double Helix Network News
Devoted to genetics and
hereditary disease in Aussies.
E-mail: helix@qnis.net

Books

ASCA Yearbooks. Available
through the ASCA.
Coile, D.C. *Show Me!* Hauppauge,
NY: Barron's Educational Series,
Inc., 1997.
Cornwell, S. *Judging the Aus-
tralian Shepherd.* 10346 E
2600 N. Rd., Potomac, IL
61865, 1991.
Hartnagle-Taylor, J. J. *All About
Aussies.* Loveland, CO: Alpine,
1996.
Holland, V.S. *Herding Dogs:
Progressive Training.* New York:
Howell, 1994.

Minstretta, V. and C. *The Struc-
ture and Movement of the
Australian Shepherd.* 3167
Dodge Rd., White City, OR
97503, 1990.
Palika, L. *The Australian Shep-
herd: Champion of Versatility.*
New York: Howell, 1995.
Taggart, M. *Sheepdog Training:
An All-Breed Approach.* Love-
land, CO: Alpine, 1991.
Templeton, J. and Mundell, M.
*Working Sheepdogs: Manage-
ment and Training.* New York:
Howell, 1992.
Scott, A. *Tails of Tailless Dogs.*
Bradenton, FL: Blue Dog
Publishing, 1998.

Videos

Australian Shepherd Standard
AKC/Video Fulfillment
5580 Centerview Drive, Ste. 200
Raleigh, NC 27606-3390
(919) 233-9767

Herding I, II, and III
Canine Training System, Ltd.
7550 W. Radcliffe Ave.
Littleton, CO 80123

Stock Dog Training
Barker Video
3711 E. 29th St.
Bryan, TX 77802
1-800-635-6144

Aussie Books and Videos
Hartnagle
13637 Hwy. 86
Kiowa, CO 80117
(303) 660-6724

INDEX

Age, 22, 99, 101–103
Aggression, 34–35
Agility, 88–89
American Kennel Club
  (AKC), 7–9, 23, 86–89,
  105–108, 109
Allergies, 56, 68
Anal sacs, 58, 71
Anatomy, 47, 50, 55, 106
Antifreeze, 67
Arthritis, 99
Artificial respiration, 74
Australian Shepherd Club
  of America (ASCA),
  7–9, 23, 85, 86, 88,
  89–90, 105–108, 109

Barking, 10, 35
Bathing, 62
Behavior problems, 32–35
Bite, 63, 105–106
Bites, 72
Bleeding, 68
Blood values, 17, 65, 66
Boarding, 97
Body language, 35
Breeder, 13, 14
Breeding caveats, 60
Brushing, 62
Burns, 68–69

Cage, 25, 27–28, 30, 32
Canine Good Citizen, 43
Cardiopulmonary
  resuscitation, 75
Castration, 31, 60
Cataracts, 15, 73
Canine Eye Registry
  Foundation (CERF),
  14
Choosing, 13–23
Cleft palate, 17
Collar, 25, 39, 93
Collie eye anomaly, 15
Collie nose, 16
Coloboma, 15
Colors, 18–19, 20–21
Come, 40–42, 43, 77
Commands, 38–43, 78,
  81
Competitions, 85–90
Conformation, 19–20, 89,
  105–108
Coughing, 71, 102
CPR, 75

Crate, 25, 27–28, 30, 32
Cushings disease, 50, 57, 72

Destructive behavior, 33–34
Diarrhea, 59, 70–71, 102
Distichiasis, 15
Down, 42, 77
Driving, 80
Drowning, 75

Ear care, 62
Ears, 106
Electrical shock, 69
Emergency care, 65–70,
  74–75
Energy, 11
Epilepsy, 16
Equipment, 25–26, 39, 78
Euthanasia, 103
Exercise pen, 25, 28, 30
Eyes, 14–16, 73, 106

Fat, 47–50
Fearfulness, 33, 34
Feeding, 45–51, 103
Feet, 98–99
Fencing, 28–29
Fleas, 54–55, 56
Fractures, 98

Gathering, 80
Genetic Disease Control in
  Animals (GDC), 14
Giardia, 59
Grooming, 62–63
Gum color, 74–75

Health checks, 19, 53
Health problems, 65–75
Hearing, 38
Heart disease, 18, 50, 71
Heartworms, 58–59
Heatstroke, 69
Heel, 42–43
Herding, 9–10, 13, 34,
  77–83, 85–86
Hereditary disorders, 14–19
Hip dysplasia, 16
History, 5–8
Hot spot, 56
Housebreaking, 29–32
Hypoglycemia, 69
Hypothermia, 69
Hypothyroidism, 18, 50,
  56–57, 71

Identification, 94
Injuries, 98–99
Intelligence, 11

Kennel cough, 59, 71
Kidney disease, 71, 102

Lameness, 98–99, 102
Leash, 25, 39, 93
Lost dog, 94
Lyme disease, 59

Mange, 55
Medicine, 73
Merle, 6, 15, 18–19, 20–21
Mites, 55

Nail care, 62–63
Nasal solar dermatitis, 16
Neutering, 60
North American Shepherd,
  8
National Stock Dog Reg-
  istry (NSDR), 7, 23
Nutrition, 46–47

Obedience, 13, 86–87
Odor, 57, 102
Orthopedic Foundation for
  Animals (OFA), 16
Older dogs, 99, 101–103
Olfaction, 87

Pain, 54
Parasites, 54–59, 70
Parvovirus, 59
Patent ductus arteriosis, 18
Pelger–Huet anomaly, 17
Pennsylvania Hip Improve-
  ment Program
  (PennHIP), 16
Poisoning, 66–67
Pressure points, 68, 70
Progressive retinal atrophy,
  15
Protein, 47
Pulse, 53–54, 75
Punishment, 31, 35
Pyoderma, 56

Quality, 22–23

Rabies, 59
Rescue organizations, 10,
  109

Retinal dysplasia, 15
Rewards, 38

Safety, 26–27, 47, 93–97
Search and rescue, 91
Seborrhea, 56
Seizures, 67
Separation anxiety,
  33
Service dogs, 91
Sex, 22, 31
Sit, 39–40
Skin problems, 56–57
Snakebites, 67–68
Spaying, 31, 60
Standard, 7–8, 89–90,
  105–108
Stay, 40, 77
Stings, 68, 72
Stock, 77, 78
Stock work, 77–83

Tail, 21
Tapeworms, 58
Taste, 46
Temperament, 8–11, 13
Temperature, 53, 75
Therapy dogs, 91
Thyroid, 18
Ticks, 54
Timing, 38
Titles, 43, 85–90
Tooth care, 63
Tracking, 87–88
Training, 37–43
Travel, 94–97

Urinary tract disease,
  71
United States Australian
  Shepherd Association
  (USASA), 7, 109

Vaccinations, 59
Veterinarian, 65
Vomiting, 70
Von Willebrandís disease,
  17

Walking, 93–94
Water, 51
Weight problems, 47–50,
  102
White, 15, 19, 20, 21
Worms, 57–58

Cover Photos

Isabelle Francais: front cover, inside front cover, inside back cover, back cover.

Photo Credits

Cindy Alison: page 33; Craig Bohren: page 92; Kent & Donna Dannen: pages 9, 20, 21, 28, 41, 57, 61, 64, 69, 72, 81, 88 (bottom left), 89, 97; Tara Darling: pages 52, 88 (top right); Isabelle Francais: pages 2–3, 4, 8, 12, 17, 29, 36, 48, 49, 56, 68, 76, 80, 84, 96, 104, 108; Pets by Paulette: pages 32, 44, 52, 100; Camille Stephens: page 24.

Important Note

This pet owner's guide tells the reader how to buy and care for an Australian Shepherd. The author and the publisher consider it important to point out that the advice given in the book is meant primarily for normally developed puppies from a good breeder—that is, dogs of excellent physical health and good character.

Anyone who adopts a fully grown dog should be aware that the animal has already formed its basic impressions of human beings. The new owner should watch the animal carefully, including its behavior toward humans, and should meet the previous owner. If the dog comes from a shelter, it may be possible to get some information on the dog's background and peculiarities there. There are dogs that, as a result of bad experiences with humans, behave in an unnatural manner or may even bite. Only people who have experience with dogs should take in such animals.

Caution is further advised in the association of children with dogs, and in exercising the dog without a leash.

Even well-behaved and carefully supervised dogs sometimes do damage to someone else's property or cause accidents. It is therefore in the owner's interest to be adequately insured against such eventualities, and we strongly urge all dog owners to purchase a liability policy that covers their dog.

About the Author

Caroline Coile is an award-winning author who has written articles about dogs for both scientific and lay publications. She holds a Ph.D. in the field of neuroscience and behavior, with special interests in canine sensory systems, genetics, and behavior. A sighthound owner since 1963, her own dogs have been nationally ranked in conformation, obedience, and field-trial competition.

© Copyright 1999 by Barron's Educational Series, Inc.

All inquiries should be addressed to:
Barron's Educational Series, Inc.
250 Wireless Boulevard
Hauppauge, NY 11788
http://www.barronseduc.com

Library of Congress Catalog Card No. 98-33445

International Standard Book No. 0-7641-0558-2

Library of Congress Cataloging-in-Publication Data
Coile, D. Caroline.
    Australian shepherds : everything about purchase, care, nutrition, behavior, and training / D. Caroline Coile.
        p.   cm. — (A complete pet owner's manual)
    Includes bibliographical references and index.
    ISBN 0-7641-0558-2 (pbk.)
    1. Australian shepherd dog. I. Title. II. Series.
SF429.A79C65   1999
636.737—dc21   98-33445
                                                        CIP

Printed in Hong Kong
9 8 7 6 5 4 3 2 1

A ussies are playful
and highly intelligent
dogs that make devoted,
protective, and loving
family companions.